BEAD FANTASIES

BEAUTIFUL, EASY-TO-MAKE JEWELRY

SAMEJIMA Takako

CONTENTS

Variations on a theme

English translation: Connie Prener

© 2003 English tex., Japan Publications Trading Co., Ltd.
English edition by Japan Publications Trading Co., Ltd., 1-2-1 Sarugaku-cho, Chiyoda-ku, Tokyo 101-0064, Japan.
First edition: First printing : August 2003

Original Japanese edition by Nihon Bungei-sha Co., Ltd., 1-7 Kanda Jinbo-cho, Chiyoda-ku, Tokyo 101-8407, Japan.

Distributors:
United States: Kodansha America, Inc. through Oxford University Press, 198 Madison Avenue, New York, NY 10016.
Canada: Fitzhenry and White Side, 195 All States Parkway, Ontario L3R 4T8.
United Kingdom and Europe: Premier Book Marketing Ltd., Claredon House, 52 Cornmarket Street, Oxford OX1 3HJ, England.
Australia and New Zealand: Bookwise International Pty Ltd. 174 Cormack Road, Wingfield, South Australia, Australia.
Asia and Japan: Japan Publications Trading Co., Ltd., 1-2-1 Sarugaku-co, Chiyoda-ku, Tokyo 101-0064, Japan.

ISBN: 4-88996-128-3
Printed in Japan

My long love affair with beads dates back to my childhood, when my grandmother made me a ring. It was just a circle of beads, but I was entranced. I began making frequent visits to the local craft store and before long, I was making my own bead jewelry. My first attempts were informed by bead books, but also involved a lot of trial and error. Over the years, my interest in beadcraft grew to the point where I now create my own designs, which I am very happy to share with you.

Each individual bead is like the paints on an artist's palette. The resulting beadwork, like a finished painting, is a reflection of its creator's individuality. I hope this book will inspire you to experience the joys of beadcraft (making and owning unique jewelry and accessories), and to create your own designs.

SAMEJIMA Takako

INTRODUCTION

Notes about the instructions in this book

Beads: Read pp. 78-79 before you begin a project. If you have difficulty finding an exact match, don't hesitate to substitute beads of the same size and shape.

Finished measurements: We have not specified finished size, since it will vary slightly according to the beads you use and how tightly you weave. Check measurements before you put the finishing touches on a piece. If adjustments are needed, increase or decrease the number of beads at an appropriate location.

Findings and other supplies: In the instructions for each project, we have specified the amount of nylon thread and/or wire you will need. For thread and wire size, see p. 80. Suggested finding sizes are on pp. 82-83.

Drawings: When it is not obvious where work begins or ends, we have supplied symbols (★ for the beginning, and ❩ for the end).

VARIATIONS ON A THEME

The pairs of pieces on the next eight pages have been made with exactly the same types of beads, but as you can see, the results are distinctly different.

ROMANTIC

CHOKER WITH ROUND FLOWER MOTIFS

Three round flower motifs, strung beads and bright blue faceted-glass bead accents combine to create this lovely, romantic choker.

★Instructions: p.12

CHOKER WITH HEPTAGONAL PENDANT

We used bugle beads to form the heptagonal pendant, and two strands of seed beads for the necklace.

★Instructions: p.13

GEOMETRIC

GRACEFUL

BRACELET WITH DIAMOND-SHAPED MOTIFS

This graceful bracelet features tiny flowers woven into diamond-shaped motifs.

★Instructions: p.14

BRACELET WITH STAR-SHAPED MOTIFS

Transparent beads are woven into star shapes to make this sparkling, elegant bracelet.

★Instructions: p.14

ELEGANT

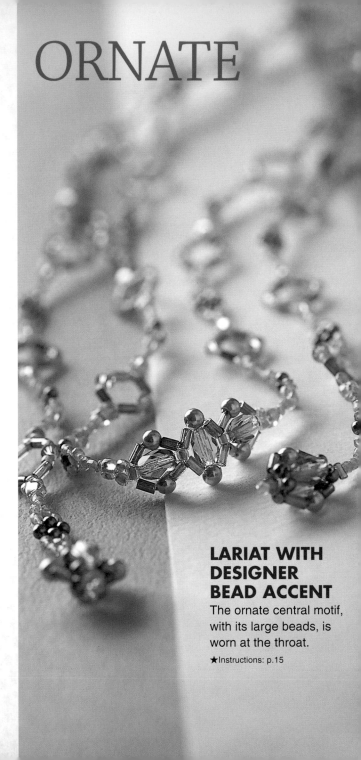

ORNATE

SIMPLE

LARIAT WITH PEARL POMPOMS

Crystal beads and pearl pompoms accent this simple design.

★Instructions: p.15

LARIAT WITH DESIGNER BEAD ACCENT

The ornate central motif, with its large beads, is worn at the throat.

★Instructions: p.15

DOME RING

Round faceted-glass and pearl beads are fashioned into a ring with a dome-shaped top.

★Instructions: p.16

MODERN

CLASSIC

PEARL RING

This ring features a wide strip of pearl beads in two colors. The faceted-glass beads at the edges of the band enhance its modern look.

★Instructions: p.16

EUROPEAN

NECKLACE WITH FLOWER PENDANT

This necklace is reminiscent of a piece you might find in an antique shop in Europe. The bead caps used in the motif add extra elegance.

★Instructions: p.16

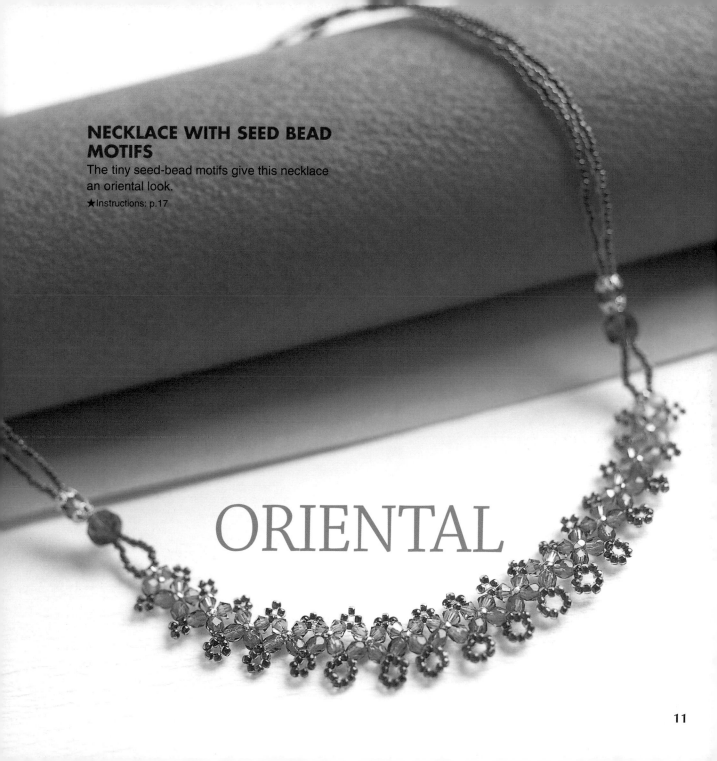

NECKLACE WITH SEED BEAD MOTIFS

The tiny seed-bead motifs give this necklace
an oriental look.

★Instructions: p.17

ORIENTAL

CHOKER WITH ROUND FLOWER MOTIFS

Supplies

A : 6 5-mm bicone crystal beads (light brown)
B : 12 3-mm bicone crystal beads (aqua)
C : 18 3-mm bicone crystal beads (green)
D : 28 3-mm bicone crystal beads (light blue)
E : 5 5-mm round fire-polished beads (blue)
F : 46 3-mm bugle beads (blue)
G : 238 1.5-mm seed beads (blue)

2 crimp beads, 2 bead tips, 4-mm jump ring, spring clasp, adjustable chain closure, nylon thread (3 40-cm lengths, 1 60-cm length)

Instructions

①Make Motifs **a** (2) and **b** (1). Tie threads; cut excess.
②String beads and motifs on nylon thread. Attach a bead tip and crimp bead to each end, then clasp and adjustable chain closure.

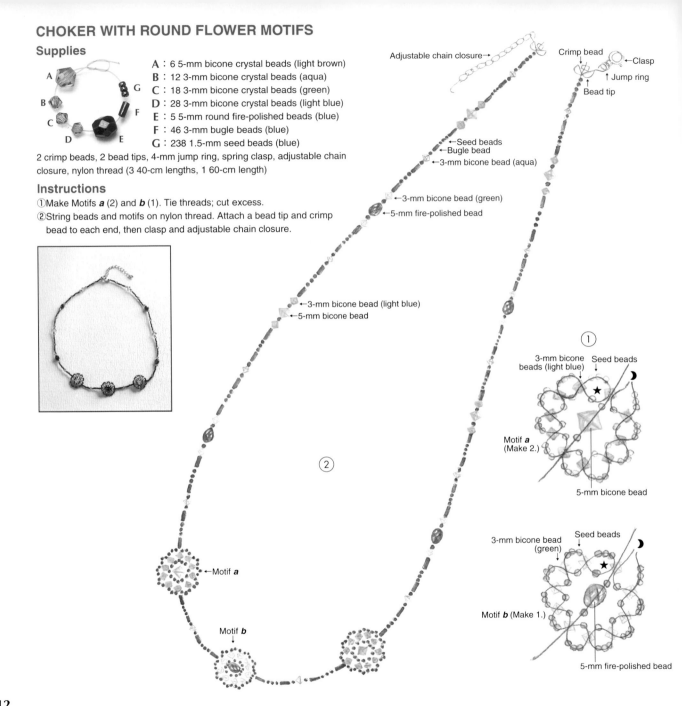

Adjustable chain closure→
Crimp bead
Clasp
↑ Jump ring
Bead tip

←Seed beads
←Bugle bead
←3-mm bicone bead (aqua)

←3-mm bicone bead (green)
←5-mm fire-polished bead

←3-mm bicone bead (light blue)
←5-mm bicone bead

②

←Motif **a**

Motif **b**

①
3-mm bicone beads (light blue)   Seed beads
★
Motif **a** (Make 2.)
5-mm bicone bead

3-mm bicone bead (green)   Seed beads
★
Motif **b** (Make 1.)
5-mm fire-polished bead

12

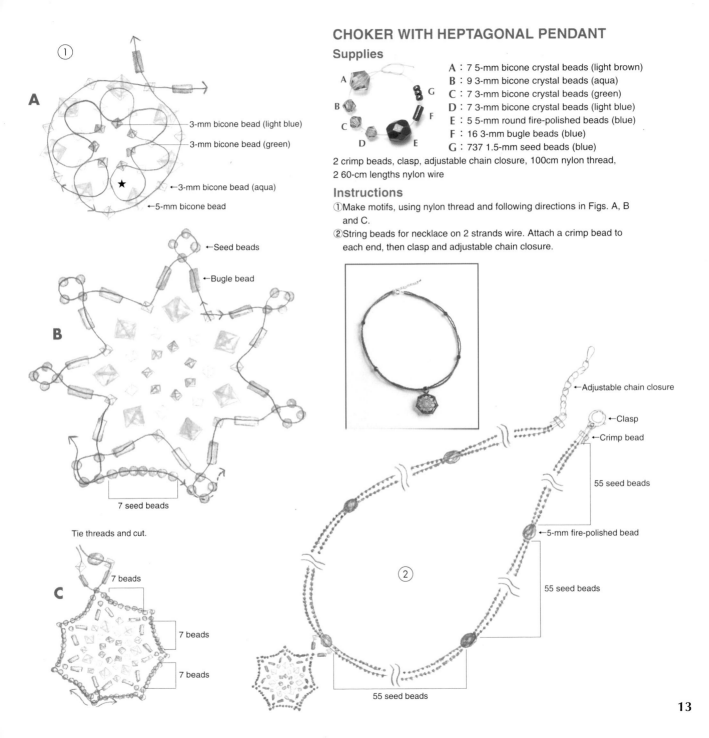

CHOKER WITH HEPTAGONAL PENDANT

Supplies

A : 7 5-mm bicone crystal beads (light brown)
B : 9 3-mm bicone crystal beads (aqua)
C : 7 3-mm bicone crystal beads (green)
D : 7 3-mm bicone crystal beads (light blue)
E : 5 5-mm round fire-polished beads (blue)
F : 16 3-mm bugle beads (blue)
G : 737 1.5-mm seed beads (blue)

2 crimp beads, clasp, adjustable chain closure, 100cm nylon thread,
2 60-cm lengths nylon wire

Instructions

①Make motifs, using nylon thread and following directions in Figs. A, B and C.

②String beads for necklace on 2 strands wire. Attach a crimp bead to each end, then clasp and adjustable chain closure.

Figure A labels:
- 3-mm bicone bead (light blue)
- 3-mm bicone bead (green)
- ←3-mm bicone bead (aqua)
- ←5-mm bicone bead

Figure B labels:
- ←Seed beads
- ←Bugle bead
- 7 seed beads

Tie threads and cut.

Figure C labels:
- 7 beads
- 7 beads
- 7 beads

Figure ② labels:
- ←Adjustable chain closure
- ←Clasp
- ←Crimp bead
- 55 seed beads
- ←5-mm fire-polished bead
- 55 seed beads
- 55 seed beads

BRACELET WITH DIAMOND-SHAPED MOTIFS

Supplies

A : 2 6-mm round faceted-glass beads (crystal)
B : 12 3-mm round faceted-glass beads (aurora crystal)
C : 28 3-mm bicone crystal beads (crystal)
D : 24 3-mm bicone crystal beads (lavender)
E : 24 3-mm bicone crystal beads (yellow)
F : 204 1.5-mm seed beads (silver)
4-mm jump ring, 2 bead tips, 2 crimp beads, spring clasp, adjustable chain closure, nylon thread (3 50-cm lengths, 2 100-cm lengths)

Instructions

①Make 3 motifs, referring to drawings. Tie threads; cut excess.

②String beads and motifs on 2 strands nylon thread, referring to drawings. Attach a bead tip and crimp bead to each end, then clasp and adjustable chain closure.

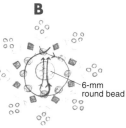

① ←Bicone bead (yellow)
←Seed bead
←Bicone beads (lavender)

②
Clasp→
Jump ring→
Crimp bead→
Bead tip
6-mm round bead
20 seed beads
10 seed beads
←3-mm bicone bead
←3-mm round bead
Adjustable chain closure→

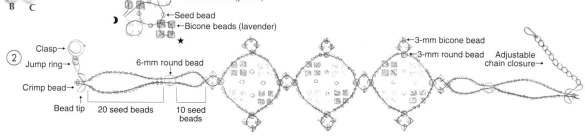

BRACELET WITH STAR-SHAPED MOTIFS

Supplies

A : 6-mm round faceted-glass bead (crystal)
B : 8 3-mm round faceted-glass beads (aurora crystal)
C : 4 3-mm bicone crystal beads (crystal)
D : 14 3-mm bicone crystal beads (lavender)
E : 20 3-mm bicone crystal beads (yellow)
F : 314 1.5-mm seed beads (silver)
4-mm jump ring, 2 bead tips, 2 crimp beads, spring clasp, adjustable chain closure, nylon thread (1 100-cm length, 2 200-cm lengths)

Instructions

①Make motifs, referring to Figs. A, B and C. Tie threads; cut excess.

②Referring to drawings, weave one side of bracelet, picking up seed beads on motif. Weave other side in same way. Attach a bead tip and crimp bead to each end, then clasp and adjustable chain closure.

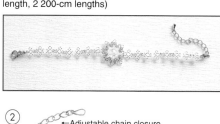

B
←6-mm round bead

C Tie threads and cut.

① **A**

←Seed beads
←Bicone bead (yellow)
Bicone bead (lavender)
3-mm round bead

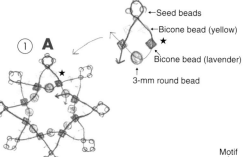

②
←Adjustable chain closure

Motif

Clasp
Jump ring

Crimp bead
Bead tip

Bicone bead (crystal)
Bicone bead (yellow)
Bicone bead (lavender)

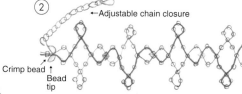

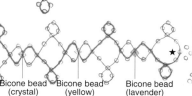

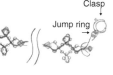

14

LARIAT WITH PEARL POMPOMS

Supplies

A : 9 4 x 6-mm designer beads (purple)
B : 8 4 x 6-mm designer beads (green)
C : 68 3-mm bicone crystal beads (light blue)
D : 52 3-mm pearl beads (light brown)
E : 42 2-mm pearl beads (brown)
F : 34 3-mm triangle beads (beige)
G : 42 3-mm bugle beads (green)
H : 358 1.8-mm three-cut beads (yellow-green)
2 crimp beads, nylon thread (2 60-cm lengths, 1 150-cm length)

Instructions

①Make 2 motifs: String beads on thread to form a circle (Fig. 1A).
Continue weaving, picking up bugle beads as you go along (Fig. 1B).
②String motifs and beads on nylon thread, referring to drawings.
Alternate between purple **(a)** and green **(b)** designer beads. Attach a
crimp bead to each end.

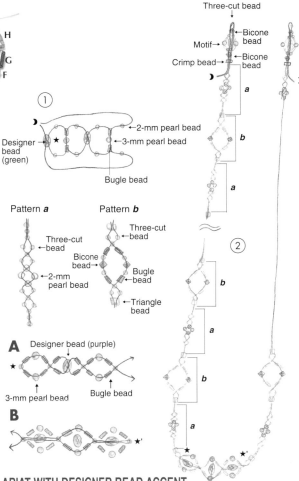

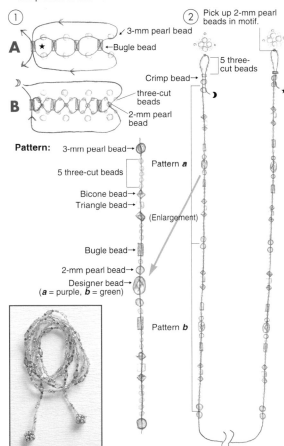

LARIAT WITH DESIGNER BEAD ACCENT

Supplies

A : 3 4 x 6-mm designer beads (purple)
B : 4 4 x 6-mm designer beads (green)
C : 44 3-mm bicone crystal beads (lavender)
D : 10 3-mm pearl beads (light brown)
E : 104 2-mm pearl beads (brown)
F : 42 3-mm triangle beads (beige)
G : 100 3-mm bugle beads (green)
H : 562 1.8-mm three-cut beads (yellow-green)
2 crimp beads, nylon thread (2 40-cm lengths, 2 160-cm lengths)

Instructions

①Make 2 motifs. Tie threads; cut excess.
②Begin weaving at ★ in Fig. A. Attach crimp bead to end. Beginning at
★' in Fig. B with separate thread, weave opposite side. Attach crimp
bead to other end.

DOME RING

Supplies

A：4 3-mm round faceted-glass beads (red)
B：4 4-mm round fire-polished beads (pink gold)
C：12 2-mm pearl beads (brown)
D：4 2-mm pearl beads (light brown)
E：68 1.5-mm seed beads (brown)
F：27 1.5-mm seed beads (silver)
100cm nylon thread

Instructions

Weave ring, referring to drawing and beginning at ★. Tie threads; cut excess.

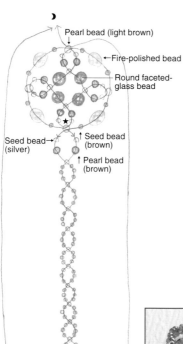

Pearl bead (light brown)
←Fire-polished bead
Round faceted-glass bead
Seed bead→ (silver)
↑ Seed bead (brown)
↑ Pearl bead (brown)

PEARL RING

Supplies

A：2 3-mm round faceted-glass beads (red)
B：2 4-mm round fire-polished beads (pink gold)
C：28 2-mm pearl beads (brown)
D：14 2-mm pearl beads (light brown)
E：7 1.5-mm seed beads (brown)
F：67 1.5-mm seed beads (silver)
100cm nylon thread

Instructions

Weave ring, referring to drawing and beginning at ★. Tie threads; cut excess.

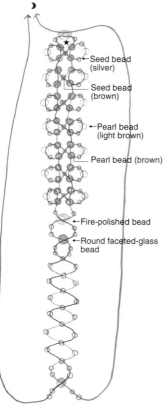

←Seed bead (silver)
Seed bead (brown)
←Pearl bead (light brown)
Pearl bead (brown)
←Fire-polished bead
Round faceted-glass bead

NECKLACE WITH FLOWER PENDANT

Supplies

A：6-mm round faceted-glass bead (blue)
B：4-mm round faceted-glass bead (aqua)
C：13 3-mm bicone crystal beads (aqua)
D：12 4-mm round fire-polished beads (purple)
E：5 3-mm round fire-polished beads (purple)
F：6 1.8-mm three-cut beads (gold)
G：371 1.5-mm seed beads (red)
H：8 bead caps (gold)
2-cm headpin, 2 2-cm eyepins, 2 crimp beads, spring clasp, adjustable chain closure, 80cm nylon thread, 80-cm nylon wire

Instructions

①Make motif, referring to Figs. A, B and C. Tie threads; cut excess.
②With wire, pick up seed beads in motif. Continue stringing beads to make necklace, referring to drawing on next page. Attach a crimp bead to each end, then clasp and adjustable chain closure.
③Insert eyepin into beads (see drawing on next page). Attach eyepin to motif.

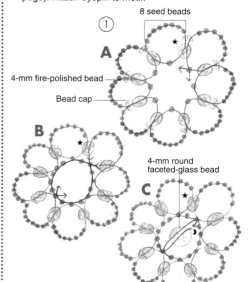

①

8 seed beads

A

4-mm fire-polished bead
Bead cap

B

4-mm round faceted-glass bead

C

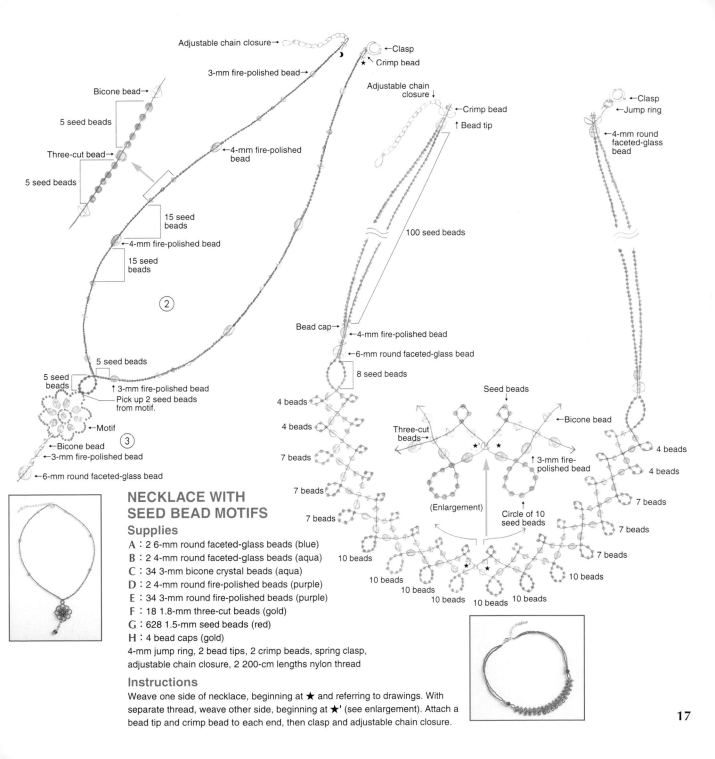

Adjustable chain closure→

3-mm fire-polished bead

Bicone bead→

5 seed beads

Three-cut bead→

5 seed beads

←4-mm fire-polished bead

15 seed beads

←4-mm fire-polished bead

15 seed beads

②

5 seed beads

5 seed beads

↑ 3-mm fire-polished bead
Pick up 2 seed beads from motif.

←Motif

③

←Bicone bead
←3-mm fire-polished bead

←6-mm round faceted-glass bead

←Clasp
★ ←Crimp bead

Adjustable chain closure ↓

←Crimp bead
↑ Bead tip

100 seed beads

Bead cap→

←4-mm fire-polished bead

←6-mm round faceted-glass bead

8 seed beads

4 beads

4 beads

7 beads

7 beads

7 beads

←Clasp
←Jump ring
←4-mm round faceted-glass bead

Seed beads

Three-cut beads→

←Bicone bead

★' ★

↑ 3-mm fire-polished bead

(Enlargement)

Circle of 10 seed beads

4 beads

4 beads

7 beads

7 beads

7 beads

10 beads

★ ★

10 beads

10 beads

10 beads

10 beads

10 beads

10 beads

NECKLACE WITH SEED BEAD MOTIFS

Supplies

A : 2 6-mm round faceted-glass beads (blue)
B : 2 4-mm round faceted-glass beads (aqua)
C : 34 3-mm bicone crystal beads (aqua)
D : 2 4-mm round fire-polished beads (purple)
E : 34 3-mm round fire-polished beads (purple)
F : 18 1.8-mm three-cut beads (gold)
G : 628 1.5-mm seed beads (red)
H : 4 bead caps (gold)
4-mm jump ring, 2 bead tips, 2 crimp beads, spring clasp, adjustable chain closure, 2 200-cm lengths nylon thread

Instructions

Weave one side of necklace, beginning at ★ and referring to drawings. With separate thread, weave other side, beginning at ★' (see enlargement). Attach a bead tip and crimp bead to each end, then clasp and adjustable chain closure.

RINGS

RIBBON RING

This ring was inspired by ribbon worked into a strip of lace. The focal point is a butterfly-shaped cluster of beads.

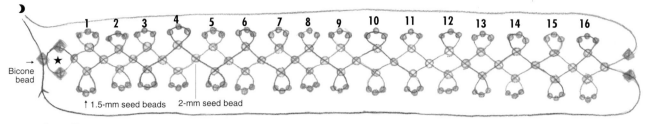

↑ 1.5-mm seed beads   2-mm seed bead

Bicone bead

Supplies

5 3-mm bicone crystal beads (red), 49 2-mm seed beads (light pink), 96 1.5-mm seed beads (red), 90-cm nylon thread

Instructions

Referring to drawings, weave beads, forming intersections. Pass thread end through first bicone bead strung to close the circle. Tie to other thread end; cut excess thread.

VARIATION

Supplies

5 3-mm bicone crystal beads (brown), 54 2-mm seed beads (beige), 108 1.5-mm seed beads (brown), nylon thread (1 100-cm length, 1 30-cm length)

Instructions

①Weave band, referring to drawings. Close circle, tie threads and cut excess.

②Picking up 2-mm seed beads from band, add 5 bicone beads, referring to drawing. Tie threads; cut excess.

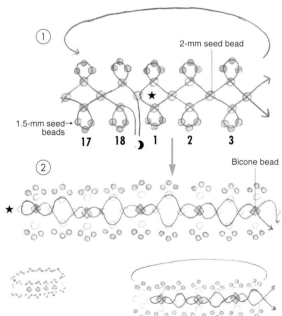

2-mm seed bead

1.5-mm seed→ beads

Bicone bead

RING WITH FACETED-GLASS BEAD FLOWER

The dark-colored beads on the band of this ring, together with the diamond-shaped flower, give this ring a contemporary look.

Supplies

8 3-mm bicone crystal beads (green), 9 4-mm round fire-polished beads (dark blue), 12 3-mm round fire-polished beads (yellow), 38 2-mm seed beads (brown), 2 50-cm lengths nylon thread

Instructions

①Make motif, referring to Figs. A and B. Tie threads; cut excess.
②Make band with separate thread, picking up seed beads in motif. Tie threads; cut excess.

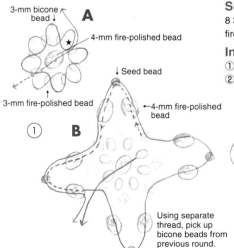

3-mm bicone bead ↓

A

4-mm fire-polished bead

↓ Seed bead

3-mm fire-polished bead

①

B

←4-mm fire-polished bead

Using separate thread, pick up bicone beads from previous round.

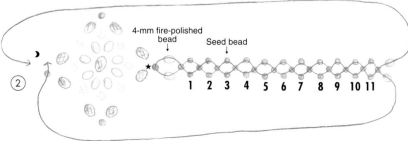

4-mm fire-polished bead

Seed bead

②

1 2 3 4 5 6 7 8 9 10 11

20

Supplies

4 4-mm round faceted-glass beads (green), 5 3-mm bicone crystal beads (light blue), 4 4-mm round fire-polished beads (bronze), 7 3-mm round fire-polished beads (green), 84 1.8-mm three-cut beads (light green), nylon thread (1 80-cm length, 1 50-cm length)

Instructions

①Make motif, referring to Figs. A, B and C. Tie threads; cut excess. Continue weaving, picking up 4-mm fire-polished beads (Fig. C). Tie threads; cut excess.

②Weave band with separate thread, referring to drawings. Tie threads; cut excess.

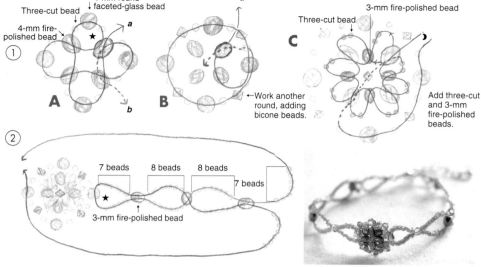

A
- Three-cut bead
- 4-mm fire-polished bead
- 4-mm round faceted-glass bead
- a
- b

B
←Work another round, adding bicone beads.

C
- Three-cut bead
- 3-mm fire-polished bead
- Add three-cut and 3-mm fire-polished beads.

②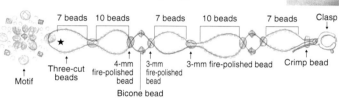

- 7 beads
- 8 beads
- 8 beads
- 7 beads
- 3-mm fire-polished bead

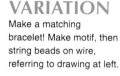

- Crimp bead
- ←Adjustable chain closure

- Motif
- Three-cut beads
- 7 beads
- 10 beads
- 7 beads
- 10 beads
- 7 beads
- Clasp
- 4-mm fire-polished bead
- 3-mm fire-polished bead
- Bicone bead
- 3-mm fire-polished bead
- Crimp bead

VARIATION

Make a matching bracelet! Make motif, then string beads on wire, referring to drawing at left.

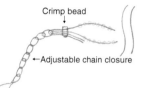

FLOWER RING

For this design, we used an unusual but striking combination of bronze and pastel beads.

RING WITH SWINGING CHARM

Supplies
5-mm round fire-polished beads (2 each gold, green and opal beige), 3 6-mm pearl beads (brown), 7 x 15-mm metal leaf bead, 193 2-mm seed beads (brown), 9 2-cm headpins, 3-mm jump ring, memory wire cut to desired length, 2-cm chain

Instructions
①String seed beads on memory wire. Round both ends with round-nose pliers.
②Attach ends of chain to ends of memory wire.
③Make ring components, referring to drawings. Attach to chain.

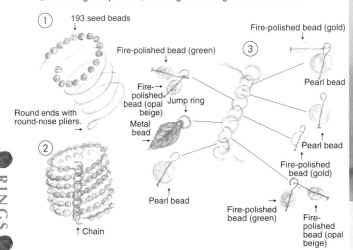

① 193 seed beads

Fire-polished bead (gold)

Fire-polished bead (green)

③

Fire-polished bead (opal beige)
Jump ring

Round ends with round-nose pliers.

Pearl bead

Metal bead

Pearl bead

②

Pearl bead

Fire-polished bead (gold)

Fire-polished bead (green)

Fire-polished bead (opal beige)

↑ Chain

GARDEN RING

Supplies
3-mm bicone crystal beads (3 red, 12 brown 18 wine), 2-mm seed beads (62 green, 80 light green), memory wire cut to desired length

Instructions
Round one end of memory wire with round-nose pliers. String beads, referring to drawings. Round other end of ring.

←Round end with round-nose pliers.

40 seed beads (light green)

★

40 seed beads (light green)

RING WITH SWINGING CHARM
To make this ring, you simply string seed beads on memory wire, which is then adorned with a charm fashioned from beads, headpins and chain.

GARDEN RING
Beads are strung on memory wire in flower and leaf patterns to make this lovely ring.

RING WITH SEED-BEAD SETTING

This exquisite ring features bicone crystal beads in an elegant seed bead setting.

Supplies

5 5-mm bicone crystal beads (aqua), 88 2-mm seed beads (silver), 70-cm nylon thread

Instructions

①Make setting components, referring to Figs. A and B.
②String beads for band. Pass thread back through beads to *d*, as shown in drawing.
③Add seed beads, picking up bicone beads as you go along. Tie threads; cut excess.

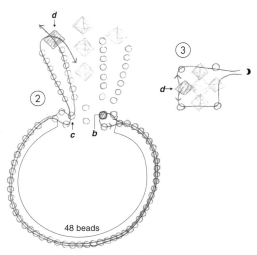

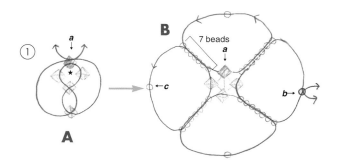

23

LACY GEMSTONE RING

Gemstone beads framed by circles of seed beads form this lacy, elegant ring.

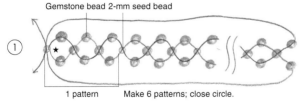

Gemstone bead 2-mm seed bead

① ★

1 pattern   Make 6 patterns; close circle.

Supplies

48 2-mm gemstone beads (red), 6 2-mm seed beads (pink silver), 168 1.5-mm seed beads (red), 100-cm nylon thread

Instructions

①Weave the 6 inner patterns, referring to drawings; close circle.
②Weave outer portion of ring (form intersections at **a**). Tie threads; cut excess.

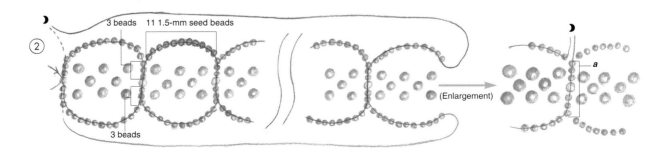

② 3 beads   11 1.5-mm seed beads

3 beads

(Enlargement)   **a**

24

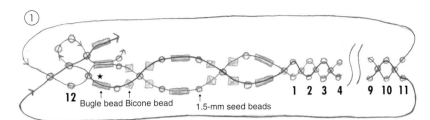

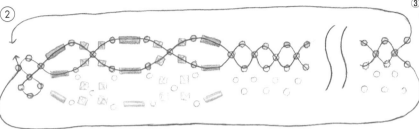

Supplies

24 3-mm bicone crystal beads (light brown), 9 6-mm bugle beads (green), 92 1.5-mm seed beads (bronze), nylon thread (1 100-cm length, 1 25-cm length)

Instructions

①Beginning at ★, weave bottom row, forming inter-sections.
②Weave top row, referring to drawings. Tie threads; cut excess.
③With separate thread, pick up bead at ★ and weave central motifs. Tie threads; cut excess.

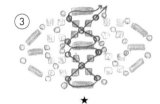

FLOWER RING

Bicone beads and long bugle beads are combined to form this beautiful flower ring.

RING WITH ROUND FIRE-POLISHED BEAD MOTIF

The beads in the large, round motif reflect light beautifully. We also include instructions for a matching bracelet.

FRESHWATER PEARL RING

This luxurious ring features an off-round freshwater pearl bead framed by faceted-glass and bicone beads.

RING WITH ROUND FIRE-POLISHED BEAD MOTIF

Supplies

4 3-mm bicone crystal beads (red), 4 5-mm round fire-polished beads (bronze), 10 3-mm round fire-polished beads (brown), 3-mm metal bead (gold), 4 2-mm seed beads (red), 73 1.5-mm seed beads (bronze), nylon thread (1 70-cm length, 1 50-cm length)

Instructions

①Weave motif, referring to Figs. A and B. Pull thread tightly, tie ends together and cut excess.

②Weave band with separate thread. Close circle, tie threads and cut excess.

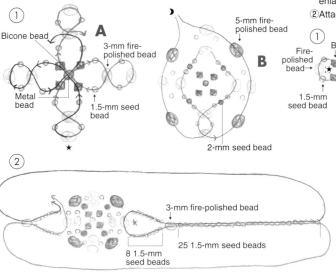

① Bicone bead / **A** / 3-mm fire-polished bead / Metal bead / 1.5-mm seed bead / ★ / **B** / 5-mm fire-polished bead / 2-mm seed bead

② 3-mm fire-polished bead / 8 1.5-mm seed beads / 25 1.5-mm seed beads

VARIATION: BRACELET

Supplies

48 3-mm bicone crystal beads (red), 48 3-mm round fire-polished beads (brown), 12 3-mm metal beads (gold), 48 2-mm seed beads (red), 118 1.5-mm seed beads (bronze), 5 5-mm jump rings, spring clasp, adjustable chain closure, 200-cm nylon thread

Instructions

①Weave 12 motifs, referring to drawings. Weave outer section (see enlargement). Tie threads; cut excess.

②Attach a jump ring at each end, then clasp and adjustable chain closure.

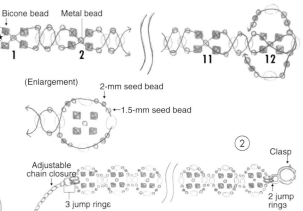

① Fire-polished bead→ / Bicone bead / Metal bead / 1.5-mm seed bead / **1** / **2** / **11** / **12**

(Enlargement) / 2-mm seed bead / ←1.5-mm seed bead

② Adjustable chain closure / 3 jump rings / Clasp / 2 jump rings

FRESHWATER PEARL RING

Supplies

6-mm off-round freshwater pearl bead (white), 4 3-mm bicone crystal beads (pink), 17 3-mm round fire-polished beads (light pink), 40 2-mm seed beads (brown), 90cm nylon thread

Instructions

Begin weaving at ★. Close circle, tie threads and cut excess. Weave motif, referring to Figs. A and B.

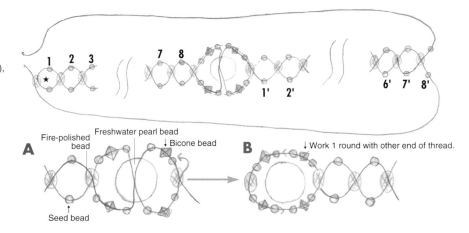

1 ★ **2 3** / **7 8** / **1' 2'** / **6' 7' 8'**

A Fire-polished bead / Freshwater pearl bead / ↓Bicone bead / Seed bead / **B** ↓Work 1 round with other end of thread.

CROSS EARRINGS

The cross-shaped motif of these monochrome earrings has a large, round bead highlight at the center.

EARRINGS

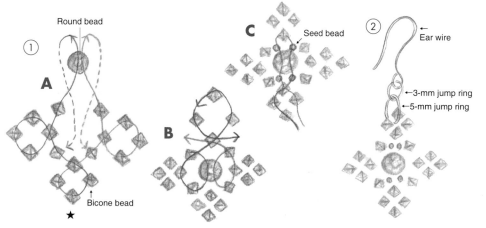

①

A Round bead

Bicone bead

B

C Seed bead

② Ear wire

←3-mm jump ring
←5-mm jump ring

Supplies

2 4-mm round faceted-glass beads (red), 40 3-mm bicone crystal beads (red), 8 2-mm seed beads (red), 2 3-mm jump rings, 2 5-mm jump rings, 2 60-cm lengths nylon thread, ear wires

Instructions

①Make motifs, referring to Figs. A and B. Add seed beads at center, as shown in Fig. C. Tie threads; cut excess.
②Attach motifs to ear wires with jump rings.

28
★

BIRDCAGE EARRINGS

Cages made of black beads surround pink and lavender "birds."

Supplies

3-mm bicone crystal beads (2 black, 2 lavender), 2 4-mm round faceted-glass beads (black), 4 4-mm round fire-polished beads (pink), 20 3-mm round fire-polished beads (black), 10 4 x 6-mm oval faceted-glass designer beads (black), 40 2-mm seed beads (black), 2 2-cm eyepins, 2 3-cm headpins, 2 80-cm lengths nylon thread, ear wires

Instructions

① Make motif. Begin weaving at ★, referring to drawings. Close circle. Add 1 round of seed beads at top and bottom. Tie threads; cut excess.

② Insert a headpin into motif, then bicone bead. Round end of headpin. Insert a round bead into an eyepin. Attach to headpin and ear wire.

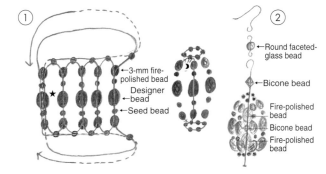

Supplies

2 4-mm bicone crystal beads (blue), 3-mm bicone crystal beads (4 blue, 20 light brown), 4 4-mm round fire-polished beads (violet), 2 6-mm round fire-polished beads (crystal), 96 2-mm seed beads (pink), 2 2-cm eyepins, 2 3-cm headpins, 2 60-cm lengths nylon thread, ear wires

Instructions

① Weave motif, beginning with the circle of beads shown in Fig. A. Add beads to perimeter (Fig. B) on one side. Insert 6-mm fire-polished bead into center. Weave opposite side. Tie threads; cut excess.

② Insert a headpin into a bicone bead, then motif, then another bicone bead. Round end of headpin. Insert an eyepin into a 4-mm bicone bead. Attach to headpin and ear wire.

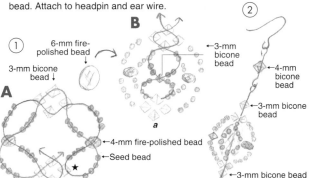

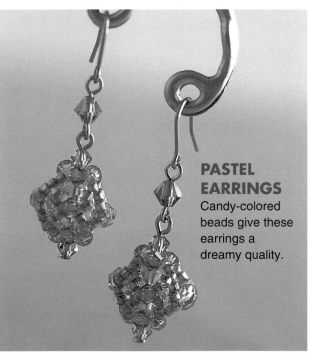

PASTEL EARRINGS

Candy-colored beads give these earrings a dreamy quality.

29

CLASSIC DANGLES

Supplies

2 6 x 8-mm freshwater pearl beads, 2 4-mm bicone crystal beads (red),
2 6-mm bugle beads (brown), 4 2-mm metal beads (gold), 4 bead caps,
4 2-cm eyepins, 2 2-cm headpins, ear wires

Instructions

Make earring components, referring to drawings. Attach to ear wires.

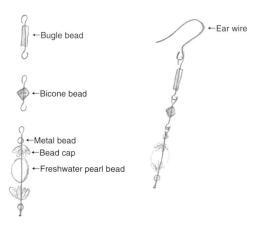

CLASSIC DANGLES
Bead caps lend a classic aura to these
freshwater pearl earrings.

GINGKO LEAF EARRINGS

Supplies

2 3-mm bugle beads (green), 2-mm seed beads (12 yellow, 20 light
green), 14 2-cm eyepins, 2 4-mm jump rings, 2 30-cm lengths nylon
thread, ear wires

Instructions

①Insert eyepins into yellow seed beads. Join with a jump ring.
②Add light-green seed beads, referring to drawing below.
③Insert eyepin into bugle bead; attach to earring and ear wire.

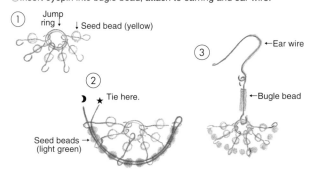

GINGKO LEAF
EARRINGS
Only seed beads and bugle
beads are used to create
these earrings, inspired by
gingko leaves.

EARRINGS

BEAD-BALL EARRINGS

To make these delicate earrings, we enclosed fire-polished beads in bead balls.

PEARL CLUSTER EARRINGS

These gorgeous earrings are simple to make, consisting only of freshwater pearl beads, headpins and jump rings.

BEAD-BALL EARRINGS

Supplies

2 4-mm round fire-polished beads (bronze), 60 1.8-mm three-cut beads (gold), 2 2-cm headpins, 2 50-cm lengths nylon thread, 2 2.5-cm lengths chain, ear wires

Instructions

①Make motif, referring to Figs. A, B and C. Tie threads; cut excess.
②Attach motifs to chain and ear wires.

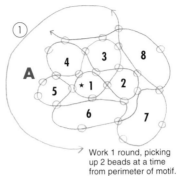

A

Work 1 round, picking up 2 beads at a time from perimeter of motif.

B Insert headpin strung with fire-polished bead.

(Side view)

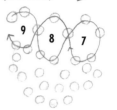

(Top view)

C

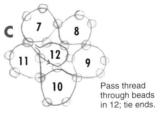

Pass thread through beads in 12; tie ends.

②

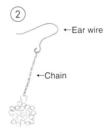

←Ear wire

←Chain

PEARL CLUSTER EARRINGS

Supplies

20 4-mm freshwater pearl beads (gray), 20 2-cm headpins, 2 3-mm jump rings, 2 5-mm jump rings, ear wires

Instructions

Make 20 components (see drawing at left below). Attach 10 to each 5-mm jump ring. Attach earrings to ear wires with 3-mm jump rings.

Parts

←Freshwater pearl bead

(Make 20.)

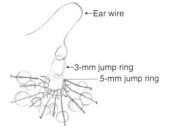

←Ear wire

←3-mm jump ring
←5-mm jump ring

E A R R I N G S

31

Supplies

2 4-mm bicone crystal beads (red), 12 4-mm round fire-polished beads (pink gold), 30 2-mm seed beads (pink gold), 2 2-cm headpins, 2 50-cm lengths nylon thread, ear wires

Instructions

①Make motif, referring to drawings. Pull thread tightly, tie ends and cut excess.

②Insert headpin into beads and motif, as shown in drawings. Insert fire-polished bead into motif. Round end of headpin.

③Attach ear wires.

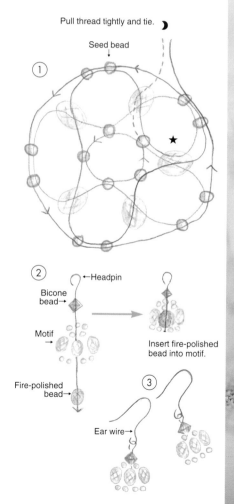

Pull thread tightly and tie.

Seed bead

① ★

②
Headpin
Bicone bead→
Motif →
Insert fire-polished bead into motif.
Fire-polished bead→

③
Ear wire→

DIADEM EARRINGS

Metallic faceted beads and bicone beads are combined to form these tiny crowns.

32

STAR EARRINGS

Two star-shaped motifs are joined together to add volume to these delicate earrings.

Supplies

3-mm round fire-polished beads (10 green, 12 light green), 2-mm seed beads (10 yellow, 12 each green and light green), 2 4-mm jump rings, 2 50-cm lengths nylon thread, ear wires.

Instructions

① String 5 light green fire-polished beads, referring to drawing.

② String seed beads, referring to drawings. Tie threads; cut excess.

③ Attach jump ring to motif and then to ear wire.

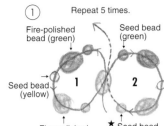

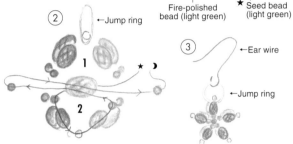

Supplies

2 4-mm bicone crystal beads (orange), 4 3-mm bicone crystal beads (green), 6 3 x 7-mm metal drop beads, 6 2-cm eyepins, 4 3-mm jump rings, ear wires

Supplies

Make earring components: 4 of **a**, and 2 of **b**. Round both ends of eyepin at a 90E angle. Attach to jump rings ands ear wires, referring to drawings.

Parts

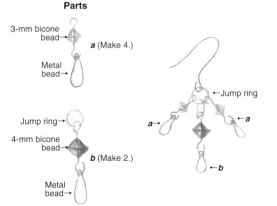

FRINGED EARRINGS

Gold drop beads form the fringe on these bright-colored earrings.

PEARL-AND-RHINESTONE EARRINGS

These dramatic earrings feature large pearl beads and rhinestones, criss-crossed by bronze seed beads.

EARRINGS

Supplies

2 2.5-mm rhinestones in Tiffany-prong settings (aurora crystal), 8 6-mm pearl beads (beige), 112 1.5-mm seed beads (bronze), nylon thread (2 100-cm lengths, 2 30-cm lengths), 12-mm perforated earring backs

Instructions

① Make motif, referring to Figs. A and B. Tie threads; cut excess.
② With separate thread, attach motif to perforated earring back. Tie threads inside earring back and cut excess.
③ Place top of perforated earring back (cut tabs in half) over bottom. Bend tabs inward with flat-nose pliers.

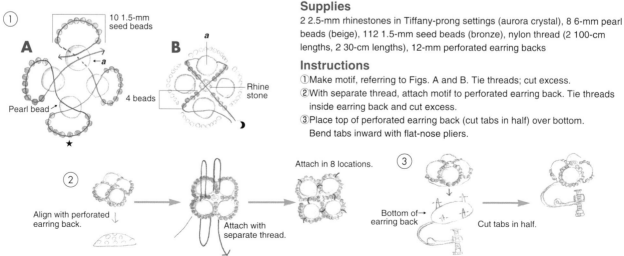

34

FLEXIBLE FLOWER EARRINGS

These earrings are designed so that the positions of the petals can be adjusted to suit your fancy.

① Parts

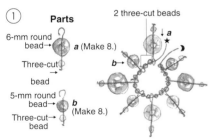

6-mm round bead→ **a** (Make 8.)

Three-cut bead

5-mm round bead→ **b** (Make 8.)

Three-cut bead

2 three-cut beads

Supplies

8 6-mm round faceted-glass beads (purple), 8 5-mm round faceted-glass beads (purple), 94 1.8-mm three-cut beads (gold), 36 1.5-mm seed beads (red), 16 2-cm headpins, nylon thread (2 20-cm lengths, 2 80-cm lengths), 12-mm perforated earring backs

Instructions

①Make **a** and **b**, referring to drawings. String three-cut beads on nylon thread, interspersing them with a and b, to complete motif. Tie threads; cut excess.

②With separate thread, attach beads to motif, referring to Figs. A, B and C. Tie threads inside perforated earring back. Cut excess.

③Place top of perforated earring back (cut tabs in half) over bottom. Bend tabs inward with flat-nose pliers.

②

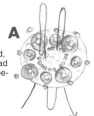

A

Work 1 round, passing thread between three-cut beads at center.

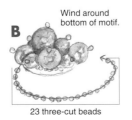

B

Wind around bottom of motif.

23 three-cut beads

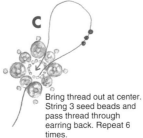

C

Bring thread out at center. String 3 seed beads and pass thread through earring back. Repeat 6 times.

③

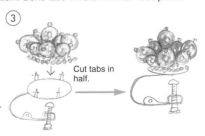

Cut tabs in half.

35

WILD ROSE BRACELET

This bracelet, with its rose motif and zigzag seed-bead band, looks beautiful from every angle.

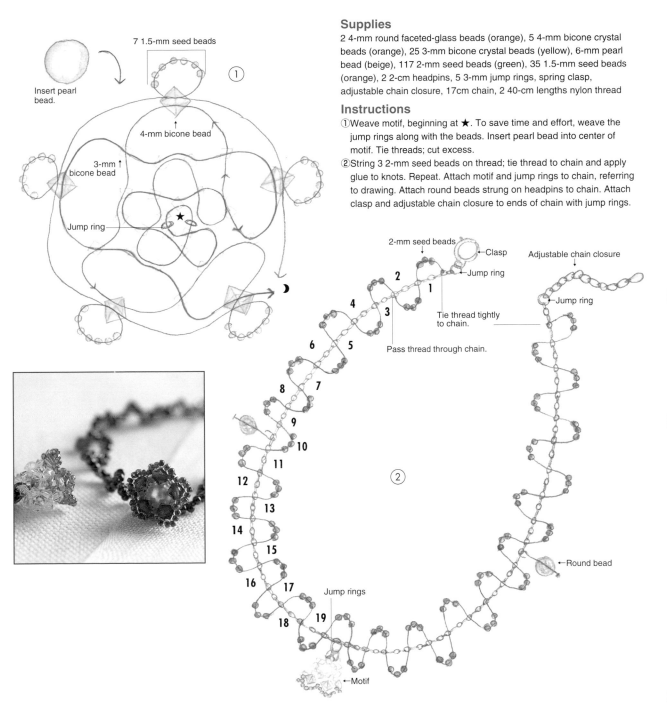

7 1.5-mm seed beads

Insert pearl bead.

①

4-mm bicone bead

3-mm ↑ bicone bead

Jump ring

Supplies

2 4-mm round faceted-glass beads (orange), 5 4-mm bicone crystal beads (orange), 25 3-mm bicone crystal beads (yellow), 6-mm pearl bead (beige), 117 2-mm seed beads (green), 35 1.5-mm seed beads (orange), 2 2-cm headpins, 5 3-mm jump rings, spring clasp, adjustable chain closure, 17cm chain, 2 40-cm lengths nylon thread

Instructions

①Weave motif, beginning at ★. To save time and effort, weave the jump rings along with the beads. Insert pearl bead into center of motif. Tie threads; cut excess.

②String 3 2-mm seed beads on thread; tie thread to chain and apply glue to knots. Repeat. Attach motif and jump rings to chain, referring to drawing. Attach round beads strung on headpins to chain. Attach clasp and adjustable chain closure to ends of chain with jump rings.

2-mm seed beads

Clasp

Jump ring

2

1

Adjustable chain closure

Jump ring

4

3

Tie thread tightly to chain.

5

6

Pass thread through chain.

7

8

9

10

11

12

②

13

14

15

Round bead

16

17

18

19

Jump rings

Motif

BRACELET WITH CYLINDRICAL MOTIF

The cylindrical motif surrounds fire-polished beads for a sophisticated, contemporary look.

Supplies

2 5-mm round fire-polished beads (gold), 24 3-mm triangle beads (orange), 32 3-mm bugle beads (purple), 120 1.8-mm three-cut beads (blue), 24 1.5-mm seed beads (blue), 2 crimp beads, spring clasp, adjustable chain closure, 2 30-cm lengths nylon wire, 50cm nylon thread

Instructions

①Weave 3 rows, referring to Figs. A and B. Add a round of 1.5-mm seed beads at top and bottom (Fig. C). Tie threads; cut excess.

②String beads and motif on 2 strands wire, referring to drawing. Attach a crimp bead at each end of bracelet, then clasp and adjustable chain closure.

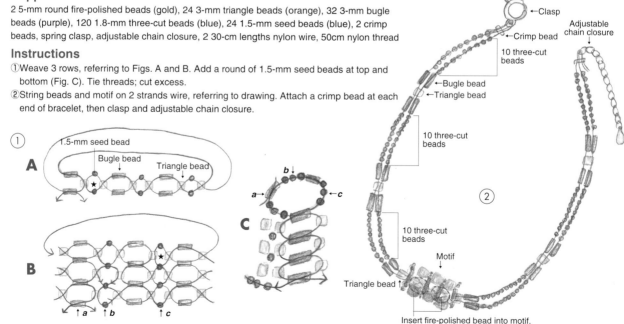

Supplies

2 6 x 8-mm oval designer beads (black), 50 3-mm bicone crystal beads (black), 26 4-mm round fire-polished beads (black), 52 3-mm round fire-polished beads (black), 54 4-mm round glass beads (black), 208 3-mm bugle beads (dark green), 654 1.5-mm seed beads (black), 2 300-cm lengths nylon thread

Instructions

Weave right side (13 rows), beginning at i. Make clasp. Tie threads; cut excess. With separate thread, pick up first bead strung. Beginning at ★' weave left side in same way.

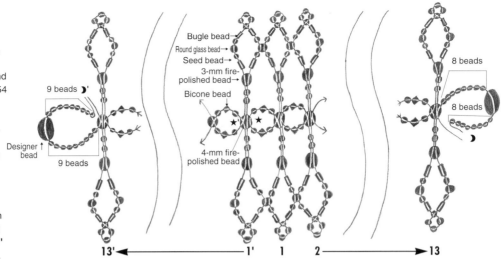

9 beads)'

Designer bead

9 beads

Bugle bead
Round glass bead→
Seed bead→
3-mm fire-polished bead→

Bicone bead

4-mm fire-polished bead

8 beads

8 beads

13' ◄———— 1' 1 2 ————► 13

BLACK LACE CUFF BRACELET

This stunning openwork bracelet combines six types of beads. Since it is woven from the center out, adjustments in size are easy to make.

NUT-AND-LEAF BRACELET

This bracelet, inspired by nature, features tiny bead nuts in addition to the leaf at its center.

Supplies

17 3 x 5-mm disc-shaped designer beads (brown), 5-mm round fire-polished bead (bronze), 18 3-mm round glass beads (gold), leaf-shaped metal beads (1 small (3.5 x 7.5mm), 1 large (8 x 14mm), 2-cm headpin, 3 4-mm jump rings, 2 crimp beads, spring clasp, adjustable chain closure, bead cap, 2 25-cm lengths nylon wire

Instructions

①Make **a**, **b** and **c**.

②String beads and components on 2 strands wire. Attach a crimp bead to each end, then clasp and adjustable chain closure.

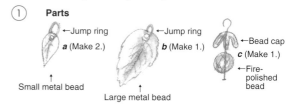

① **Parts**

←Jump ring
a (Make 2.)
↑ Small metal bead

←Jump ring
b (Make 1.)
↑ Large metal bead

←Bead cap
c (Make 1.)
←Fire-polished bead

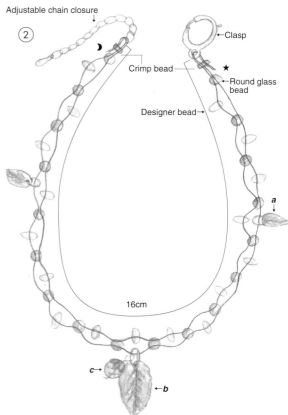

②

Adjustable chain closure

Crimp bead

←Clasp

★

←Round glass bead

Designer bead→

16cm

a

c→

←**b**

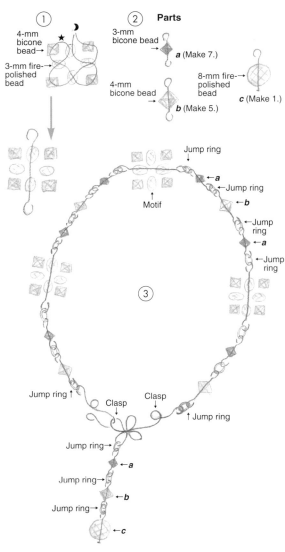

① 4-mm bicone bead→ · 3-mm fire-polished bead→

② Parts
3-mm bicone bead→ **a** (Make 7.)
4-mm bicone bead→ **b** (Make 5.)
8-mm fire-polished bead→ **c** (Make 1.)

Jump ring
←**a**
←Jump ring
←**b**
←Jump ring
←**a**
←Jump ring
Motif
③
Jump ring ↑
Clasp
Clasp
↑ Jump ring
Jump ring→
←**a**
Jump ring→
←**b**
Jump ring→
←**c**

FLOWER BRACELET WITH AN ANTIQUE LOOK

A flower-shaped connector on the clasp echoes the floral theme of this bracelet, which intersperses beads strung on eyepins and flower motifs.

Supplies

17 4-mm bicone crystal beads (green), 7 3-mm bicone crystal beads (emerald green), 8-mm round fire-polished bead (light green), 12 3-mm round fire-polished beads (yellow), 2-cm headpin, 15 2-cm eyepins, 17 4-mm jump rings, clasp set, 3 30-cm lengths nylon thread

Instructions

①Make 3 motifs; insert eyepin into each.
②Make **a**, **b** and **c**.
③Join motifs, eyepins and clasp with jump rings.

WRISTWATCH-STYLE BRACELET

The central motif was inspired by the face of a wristwatch. We chose a simple design for the band.

① A
Fire-polished bead (light blue)
Seed bead
Fire-polished bead (yellow)
★
a

B
Seed bead
3-mm round faceted-glass bead
a

Supplies

2 4-mm round faceted-glass beads (red), 6 3-mm round faceted-glass beads (red), 3-mm round fire-polished beads (14 yellow, 26 light blue), 210 1.5-mm seed beads (brown), 2 crimp beads, clasp set, 100cm nylon thread, 2 30-cm lengths nylon wire

Instructions

①Weave motif with nylon thread (Fig. A). Add seed beads and 3-mm round faceted-glass beads (Fig. B). Tie threads; cut excess.

②Make band, using wire and picking up fire-polished beads at sides of motif. Attach a crimp bead at each end, then clasp.

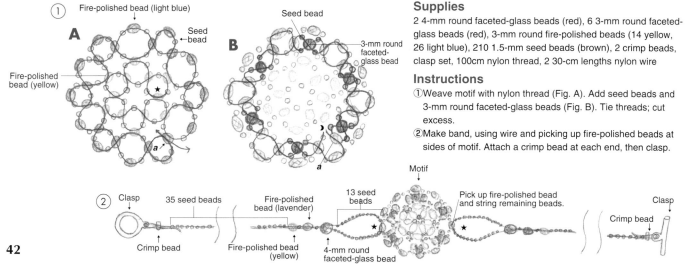

② Clasp
35 seed beads
Fire-polished bead (lavender)
13 seed beads
Motif
Pick up fire-polished bead and string remaining beads.
Clasp
Crimp bead
Crimp bead
Fire-polished bead (yellow)
4-mm round faceted-glass bead
★
★

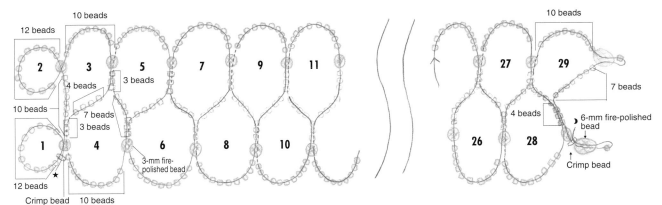

Supplies

2 6-mm round fire-polished beads (light green), 28 3-mm round fire-polished beads (light green), 1.8-mm three-cut beads (199 yellow, 296 light green), 2 crimp beads, 80cm nylon thread

Instructions

Begin weaving at ★. When first circle is completed, add a crimp bead and compress. Continue weaving until you have made all 29 circles (see drawings). Add a crimp bead, compress and cut excess thread.

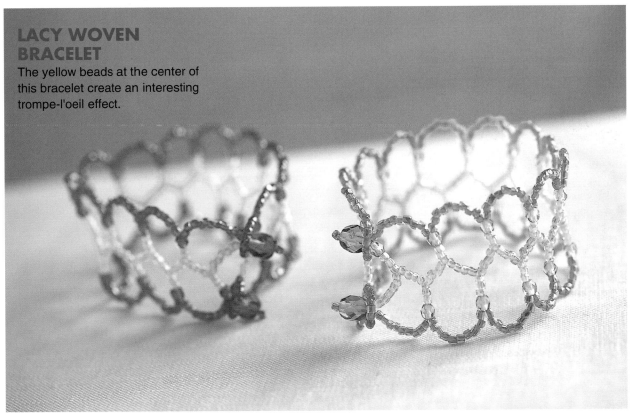

LACY WOVEN BRACELET

The yellow beads at the center of this bracelet create an interesting trompe-l'oeil effect.

Supplies

6 4-mm bicone crystal beads (rust), 4 3-mm bicone crystal beads (green), 2 5-mm round fire-polished beads (blue), 12 3-mm round fire-polished beads (purple), 12 2-mm seed beads (pink silver), 12 3-mm bugle beads (purple), 8 2 x 12-mm twisted bugle beads (purple), 8 5 x 7-mm freshwater pearl beads (purple), 2 designer spacers, 40 2-cm eyepins, 10 5-mm jump rings, 4 2.5-cm lengths chain, clasp set

Instructions

Make and assemble bracelet components. To ensure that all strands are of uniform length, begin with the outer strands, which contain the most components.

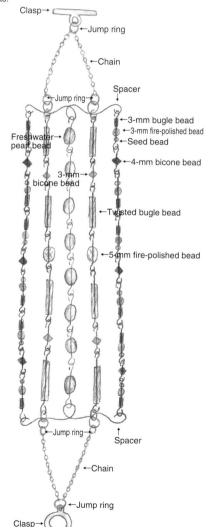

FIVE-STRAND BRACELET

Designer spacers are used to connect the strands of this stylish bracelet.

Supplies

1-cm (long) designer drop bead (purple), 24 3 x 5-mm disc-shaped designer beads (lavender), 24 4-mm round fire-polished beads (24 purple, 24 pink gold), 3-mm round fire-polished beads (24 purple, 24 light brown), 24 3-mm seed beads (bronze), 125 2-mm seed beads (pink silver), 400-cm nylon thread

Instructions

① Begin weaving at ★. For motifs, weave 1-3 (Fig. A), then weave 4-11 around 2 (Fig. B). Repeat.

② After completing 6 motifs, weave clasp (Fig. C). Tie threads; cut excess.

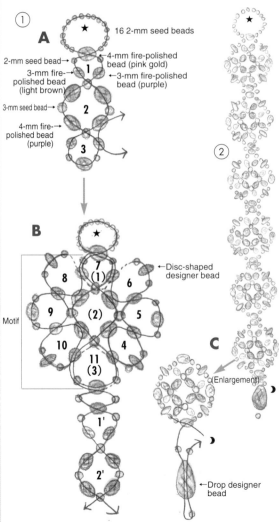

A

① ★ 16 2-mm seed beads

2-mm seed bead → ← 4-mm fire-polished bead (pink gold)

3-mm fire-polished bead (light brown) → 1 ← 3-mm fire-polished bead (purple)

3-mm seed bead → 2

4-mm fire-polished bead (purple) → 3

B ★

8 7 (1) 6 ← Disc-shaped designer bead

Motif 9 (2) 5

10 4

11 (3)

1'

2'

C (Enlargement)

← Drop designer bead

WIDE BRACELET WITH ROUND MOTIFS

Beads in a variety of shapes and colors add up to a dazzling bracelet, woven with only one strand of nylon thread.

BUTTERFLY NECKLACE

The shimmering butterfly motif is adorned with two long strands of fringe, which sway when you move.

Supplies

4-mm bicone crystal beads (12 light green, 16 green), 10 3-mm bicone crystal beads (blue), 6 4-mm round fire-polished beads (purple), 2-mm seed beads (10 light green, 12 green), 780 1.5-mm seed beads (green), 2 2-cm headpins, 6 2-cm eyepins, jump rings (1 3-mm, 2 4-mm), 2 bead tips, 2 crimp beads, spring clasp, adjustable chain closure, nylon thread (1 40-cm length, 1 30-cm length, 2 100-cm lengths)

Instructions

①Weave butterfly motif, beginning at center and working toward right (Fig. A). Tie threads; cut excess. With separate thread, weave left side (Fig. B). Tie threads; cut excess.

②Make necklace, picking up beads from motif. Attach a bead tip and crimp bead to each end, then clasp and adjustable chain closure.

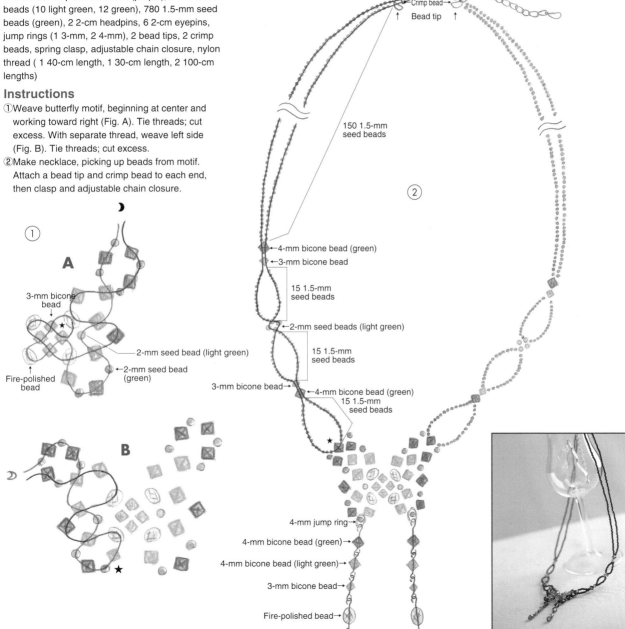

① ②

A

3-mm bicone bead

2-mm seed bead (light green)

←2-mm seed bead (green)

Fire-polished bead

B

Clasp

3-mm jump ring→

Crimp bead→

Bead tip

Adjustable chain closure

150 1.5-mm seed beads

←4-mm bicone bead (green)

←3-mm bicone bead

15 1.5-mm seed beads

←2-mm seed beads (light green)

15 1.5-mm seed beads

3-mm bicone bead→ ←4-mm bicone bead (green)
15 1.5-mm seed beads

4-mm jump ring→

4-mm bicone bead (green)→

4-mm bicone bead (light green)→

3-mm bicone bead→

Fire-polished bead→

BLUE GEMSTONE NECKLACE

This delicate two-strand necklace features gemstone bead accents.

NECKLACE WITH LILY-OF-THE-VALLEY BEAD ACCENTS

This Y-shaped necklace looks wonderful worn like a choker, with the end threaded through the loop.

NECKLACE WITH LILY-OF-THE-VALLEY BEAD ACCENTS

Supplies

3-mm round faceted-glass beads (1 pink, 1 red), 4-mm bicone crystal beads (2 green, 15 red), 3-mm round fire-polished beads (15 green, 16 purple), 2 12-mm lily-of-the-valley designer beads, 108 3-mm bugle beads (purple), 31 6-mm bugle beads (brown), 157 2-mm seed beads (green), 2 crimp beads, 150-cm nylon wire

Instructions

Make Y-shaped section, beginning at ★. Add crimp bead; compress. String beads for remainder of necklace, ending with a crimp bead.

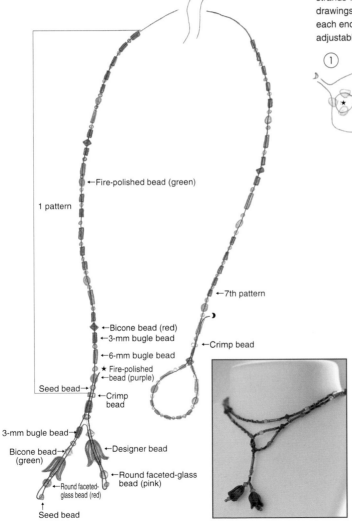

←Fire-polished bead (green)

1 pattern

←7th pattern

←Bicone bead (red)
←3-mm bugle bead
←6-mm bugle bead
★ Fire-polished
←bead (purple)
←Crimp bead

←Crimp bead

Seed bead→

3-mm bugle bead→

Bicone bead→
(green)
←Designer bead

←Round faceted-glass
bead (pink)

←Round faceted-
glass bead (red)

Seed bead

BLUE GEMSTONE NECKLACE

Supplies

34 5-mm gemstone beads (blue), 20 3-mm round fire-polished beads (aqua), 1.8-mm three-cut beads (20 yellow-green, 290 aqua), 2 crimp beads, spring clasp, adjustable chain closure, 2 30-cm lengths nylon thread, 2 60-cm lengths nylon wire

Instructions

①Make 2 motifs, using nylon thread and referring to drawings. Tie threads; cut excess.

②String beads and motifs on 2 strands wire, referring to drawings. Attach crimp bead to each end, then clasp and adjustable chain closure.

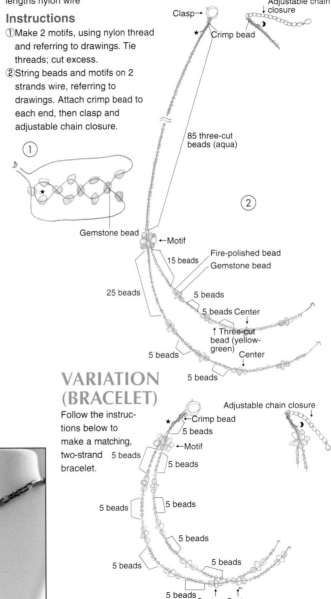

Clasp→

Adjustable chain closure

★ Crimp bead

①

85 three-cut beads (aqua)

②

Gemstone bead

←Motif

Fire-polished bead
15 beads
Gemstone bead

25 beads

5 beads
5 beads Center

↑ Three-cut bead (yellow-green)

5 beads

Center

5 beads

VARIATION (BRACELET)

Follow the instructions below to make a matching, two-strand bracelet.

Adjustable chain closure

★ Crimp bead
5 beads
←Motif
5 beads
5 beads

5 beads
5 beads

5 beads
5 beads

5 beads
5 beads

5 beads
5 beads

5 beads
Center   Center

LARIAT WITH AN OLD-FASHIONED LOOK

Drop beads enclosed by bugle beads grace
this beautiful lariat with its warm colors.

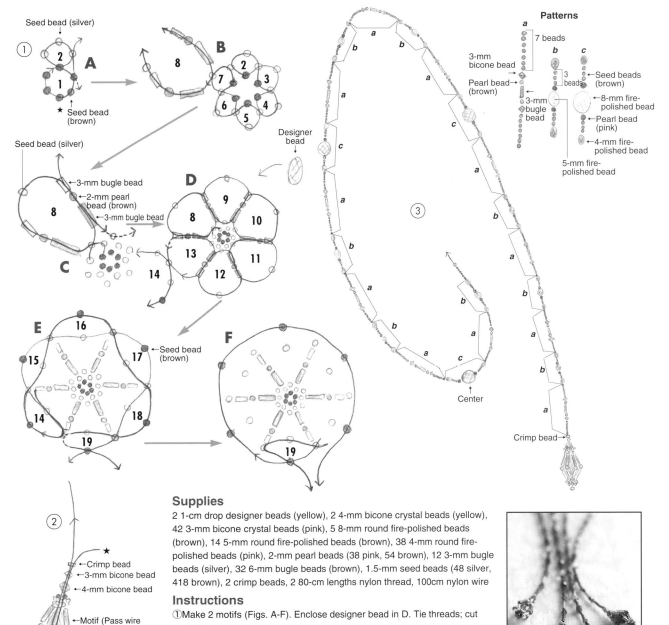

Patterns

① Seed bead (silver)

② ①

★ Seed bead (brown)

A

B
8 / 2 7 3 6 4 5

Designer bead

Seed bead (silver)
←3-mm bugle bead
←2-mm pearl bead (brown)
←3-mm bugle bead

C 8

D
9 8 10 13 11 12 14

E
16 15 17 14 18 19
←Seed bead (brown)

F
19

③

a / b / b / a / a / c / c / a / a / b / b / a / b / b / a / c

Center

Crimp bead

a
7 beads
3-mm bicone bead
Pearl bead (brown)
3-mm bugle bead

b
3 beads

c
←Seed beads (brown)
←8-mm fire-polished bead
←Pearl bead (pink)
←4-mm fire-polished bead

5-mm fire-polished bead

② ★
←Crimp bead
←3-mm bicone bead
←4-mm bicone bead
←Motif (Pass wire th-rough designer bead inside motif.)
←Pearl bead (brown)

Supplies
2 1-cm drop designer beads (yellow), 2 4-mm bicone crystal beads (yellow), 42 3-mm bicone crystal beads (pink), 5 8-mm round fire-polished beads (brown), 14 5-mm round fire-polished beads (brown), 38 4-mm round fire-polished beads (pink), 2-mm pearl beads (38 pink, 54 brown), 12 3-mm bugle beads (silver), 32 6-mm bugle beads (brown), 1.5-mm seed beads (48 silver, 418 brown), 2 crimp beads, 2 80-cm lengths nylon thread, 100cm nylon wire

Instructions
①Make 2 motifs (Figs. A-F). Enclose designer bead in D. Tie threads; cut excess.
②String beads and motifs on one end of wire. Attach crimp bead and compress.
③String beads, forming Patterns *a*, *b* and *c*, and referring to drawing. Work left and right sides in mirror image. At other end, work Step 2 in reverse. Add a crimp bead and compress.

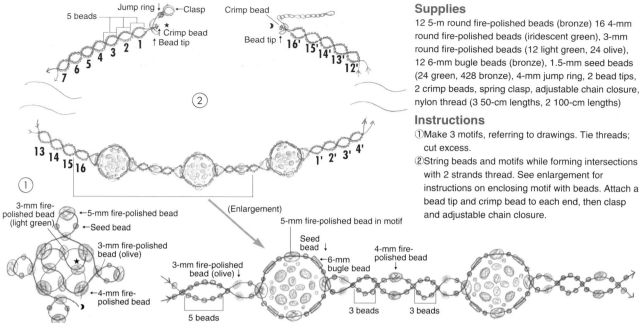

Supplies

12 5-m round fire-polished beads (bronze) 16 4-mm round fire-polished beads (iridescent green), 3-mm round fire-polished beads (12 light green, 24 olive), 12 6-mm bugle beads (bronze), 1.5-mm seed beads (24 green, 428 bronze), 4-mm jump ring, 2 bead tips, 2 crimp beads, spring clasp, adjustable chain closure, nylon thread (3 50-cm lengths, 2 100-cm lengths)

Instructions

①Make 3 motifs, referring to drawings. Tie threads; cut excess.

②String beads and motifs while forming intersections with 2 strands thread. See enlargement for instructions on enclosing motif with beads. Attach a bead tip and crimp bead to each end, then clasp and adjustable chain closure.

CHOKER WITH DIAMOND-SHAPED MOTIFS

Multidimensional diamond-shaped motifs are the highlights of this bronze and green choker.

RIBBON CHOKER

Drop and bicone beads are suspended from a length of lacy ribbon to create this piece, which is reminiscent of the Victorian era.

Center

①

5-mm jump ring→
3-mm jump ring↑

Bicone bead→

3.5-cm chain

2-cm chain

1-cm chain →

←5-mm jump ring
←3-mm jump ring

→Fire-polished bead

←Metal bead
←Designer bead

←Metal bead

←Designer bead

2-cm chain

②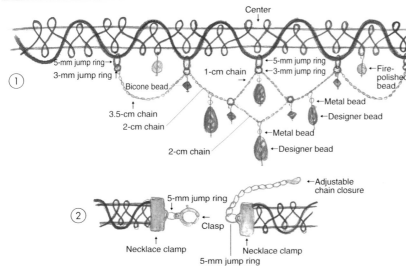

5-mm jump ring

←Clasp

Necklace clamp

5-mm jump ring

Necklace clamp

←Adjustable chain closure

Supplies

4 7-mm drop designer beads (red), 4 4-mm bicone crystal beads (red), 2 5-mm round fire-polished beads (bronze), 4 2-mm metal beads (gold), 10 2-cm headpins, jump rings (7 3-mm, 7 5-mm), 2 necklace clamps, spring clasp, adjustable chain closure, 30cm 1.5-cm ribbon (red), chain (2 3.5-cm lengths, 3 2-cm lengths, 2 1-cm lengths)

Instructions

①Join beads strung on headpins and chain, referring to drawings. Attach to ribbon.
②Insert ends of ribbon into necklace clamps. Attach clasp and adjustable chain closure with jump rings.

53

Supplies

10 4-mm bicone crystal beads (purple), 11 3-mm bicone crystal beads (green), 7 x 10-mm designer drop bead (purple), 10 flower-shaped metal connectors, 18 2-mm seed beads (pink gold), 6 4-mm jump rings, 11 2-cm headpins, 14 2-cm eyepins, spring clasp, adjustable chain closure, chain (4 13.5-cm lengths, 4 2-cm lengths, 10 2.5-cm lengths)

Instructions

①Make components (*a*, *b*, *c*, *d*, *e*).

②Connect components and chain, referring to drawings. Attach a jump ring to each end, then clasp and adjustable chain closure.

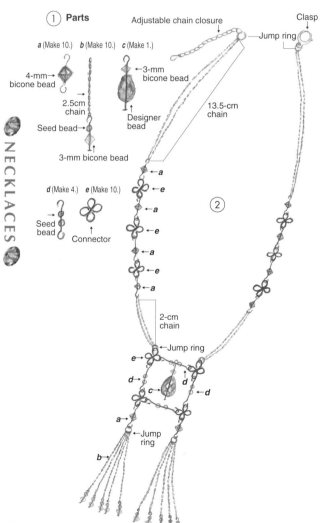

NECKLACES

① **Parts**

a (Make 10.) *b* (Make 10.) *c* (Make 1.)

4-mm bicone bead

2.5cm chain

Seed bead

3-mm bicone bead

3-mm bicone bead

Designer bead

Adjustable chain closure

Clasp

Jump ring

13.5-cm chain

d (Make 4.) *e* (Make 10.)

Seed bead

Connector

←*a*
←*e*
←*a*
←*e*
←*a*
←*e*
←*a*

2-cm chain

Jump ring

e→
d→
a→
c→
d
←*d*

Jump ring

b→

②

FRINGED NECKLACE WITH SQUARE MOTIF

The striking central motif, with its single designer bead and flower connectors, is set off by chain fringe.

FRINGED LARIAT

Beads and chain combine to make this lariat, decorated with bead-and-chain fringe.

Supplies

22 3-mm bicone crystal beads (green), 8 5-mm round fire-polished beads (iridescent green), 21 3-mm round fire-polished beads (iridescent green), 6 5 x 7-mm drop designer beads (green), 22 2-mm seed beads (green), 17 2-cm eyepins, 22 2-cm headpins, 2 4-mm jump rings, chain (12 1-cm lengths, 10 2-cm lengths, 10 4.5-cm lengths)

Instructions

①Make components (*a-h*).
②Connect components and chain, referring to drawings.

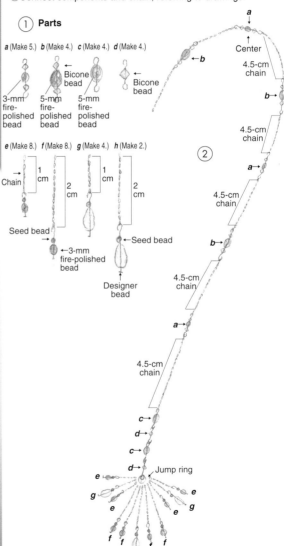

① **Parts**

a (Make 5.) *b* (Make 4.) *c* (Make 4.) *d* (Make 4.)

3-mm fire-polished bead
5-mm fire-polished bead
← Bicone bead
5-mm fire-polished bead
← Bicone bead

e (Make 8.) *f* (Make 8.) *g* (Make 4.) *h* (Make 2.)

Chain — 1 cm
2 cm
1 cm
2 cm
Seed bead
←3-mm fire-polished bead
Seed bead
Designer bead

②

a
Center
4.5-cm chain
← *b*
b →
4.5-cm chain
a →
4.5-cm chain
b →
4.5-cm chain
a →
4.5-cm chain
c →
d →
c →
d → Jump ring
e
g
e
e
g
e
f *f* *f* *f*
h

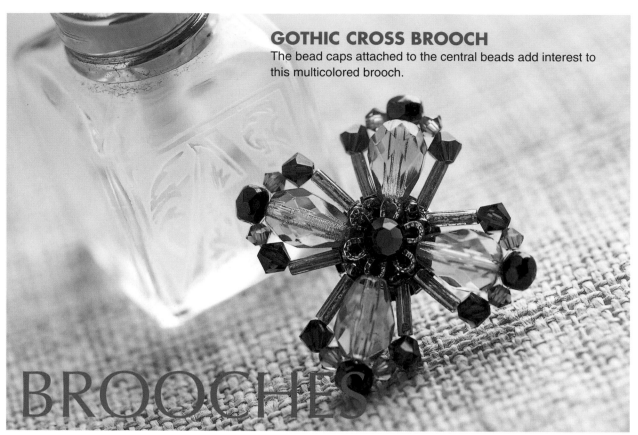

GOTHIC CROSS BROOCH
The bead caps attached to the central beads add interest to this multicolored brooch.

Supplies
4 1-cm (length) drop designer beads (yellow), 4-mm rhinestone with flat back (brown), 8 4-mm bicone crystal beads (dark blue), 8 3-mm bicone crystal beads (purple), 4 4-mm round fire-polished beads (bronze), 8 6-mm bugle beads (green), 8 2-mm seed beads (green), bead cap, nylon thread (1 80-cm length, 1 30-cm length), 12-mm (diameter) perforated pin back, glue

Instructions
① Make motif, referring to Figs. A and B. Tie threads; cut excess.
② Place motif on top of perforated pin back and attach with nylon thread (Figs. C and D).
③ Attach bead cap to center of pin back. Tie threads on inside of pin back; cut excess. Glue rhinestone to center of bead cap.
④ Cut tabs on base of pin back in half. Join top and bottom of pin back, bending tabs inward with flat-nose pliers.

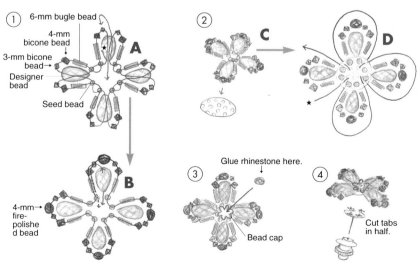

① 6-mm bugle bead
4-mm bicone bead
3-mm bicone bead→
Designer bead
Seed bead
A

② C D
★

③ B
4-mm→ fire-polished bead

③ Glue rhinestone here.
Bead cap

④ Cut tabs in half.

FOUR-LEAF CLOVER BROOCH

Stainless-steel wire is used to retain the shape of this lovely brooch, which we're sure will bring you good luck.

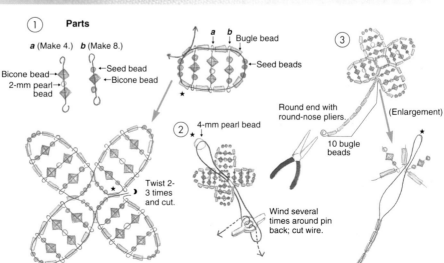

Supplies

16 4-mm bicone crystal beads (green), 4-mm pearl bead (white), 4 2-mm pearl beads (white), 38 3-mm bugle beads (green), 40 2-mm seed beads (green), 12 2-cm eyepins, stainless-steel wire (1 80-cm length, 2 30-cm lengths), 17-mm pin back

Instructions

① Make a and b, then join to form motif, referring to drawings.

② String pearl bead on separate wire. Insert into center of motif. Wrap around pin back several times to secure.

③ Insert remaining strand of wire into motif. String beads for stem. Cut wire, leaving a 15-mm end. Round end with round-nose pliers.

① **Parts**

a (Make 4.) **b** (Make 8.)

Bicone bead→
2-mm pearl→
bead

←Seed bead
←Bicone bead

a b Bugle bead

←Seed beads

Twist 2-3 times and cut.

② 4-mm pearl bead

Round end with round-nose pliers.

Wind several times around pin back; cut wire.

③

10 bugle beads

(Enlargement)

57

BLACK SNOWFLAKE BROOCH

Black beads lend a new look to this traditional, hexagonal pattern.

Supplies

6-mm round faceted-glass bead (black), 6 4-mm round faceted-glass beads (black), 48 3-mm bicone crystal beads (black), 6 3-mm bugle beads (black), 12 2-mm seed beads (black), nylon thread (7 30-cm lengths, 1 50-cm length), 15-mm (diameter) perforated pin back

Instructions

①Make 6 motifs (Figs. A, B). Tie threads; cut excess.
②Add more beads, picking up bicone beads from motifs. Tie threads; cut excess.
③Place motifs on perforated pin back. Attach with separate thread.
④Make a circle of bugle beads. Attach to pin back.
⑤Attach 6-mm bead to center of pin back. Tie thread end to thread from beginning of work inside pin back.
⑥Cut tabs on base of pin back in half. Attach top and bottom of pin back with flat-nose pliers.

A ① 4-mm round bead

Bicone bead

B

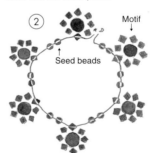

② Motif

Seed beads

④ 6 bugle beads

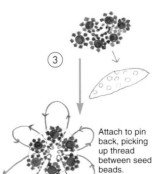

③ Attach to pin back, picking up thread between seed beads.

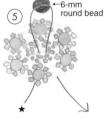

⑤ 6-mm round bead

⑥ Cut tabs in half.

Supplies

3-mm bicone crystal beads (9 light blue, 18 purple), 5-mm round fire-polished beads (1 lavender, 1 brown), 4-mm round fire-polished beads (6 green, 11 brown, 17 purple, 17 red), 11 6-mm bugle beads (brown), 2 2-cm headpins, 20 2-cm eyepins, 2 100-cm lengths nylon thread, perforated pin backs (1 15-mm, 1 22-mm)

Instructions

①Attach beads to 15-mm perforated pin back (Figs. A-C). Tie threads inside pin back; cut excess. Insert headpin into pin back from inside; round end. Cut tabs on base of pin back in half. Attach top to base with flat-nose pliers.

②Attach beads for larger brooch to 22-mm pin back (Figs. *a-d*). Follow directions in Step 1.

③Attach a and b to headpins extending from pin back.

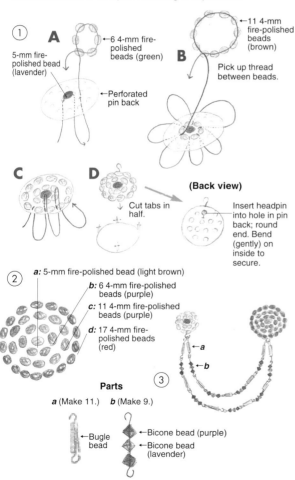

① **A**
5-mm fire-polished bead (lavender)
←6 4-mm fire-polished beads (green)
←Perforated pin back

B
←11 4-mm fire-polished beads (brown)
Pick up thread between beads.

C

D
↓ Cut tabs in half.

(Back view)
Insert headpin into hole in pin back; round end. Bend (gently) on inside to secure.

② *a:* 5-mm fire-polished bead (light brown)
b: 6 4-mm fire-polished beads (purple)
c: 11 4-mm fire-polished beads (purple)
d: 17 4-mm fire-polished beads (red)

③ ←*a*
←*b*

Parts

a (Make 11.)   *b* (Make 9.)

←Bugle bead
←Bicone bead (purple)
←Bicone bead (lavender)

DOUBLE BROOCH

Two round motifs (one large and one small) are joined by a two-strand bead chain.

59

FIGURE-EIGHT CELL PHONE STRAPS

FIGURE-EIGHT CELL PHONE STRAPS
The straps on the next page feature beads of several types and sizes woven into figure-eight patterns.

CELL PHONE STRAPS

RED STRAP

Supplies

30 3-mm bicone crystal beads (wine), 12 4-mm round fire-polished beads (red), 7 2-mm pearl beads (beige), 2-mm seed beads (32 pink silver, 32 light pink), bead tip, crimp bead, 2 50-cm lengths nylon thread, purchased strap

Instructions

Weave figure eights with 2 strands nylon thread, referring to drawing. Attach a bead tip to all 4 strands at end. Secure with a bead tip and crimp bead; attach purchased strap.

Purchased→
strap

Crimp bead
↓

Bead tip→

Seed bead
←(light pink)

←Seed bead
(pink silver)

↓ Bicone bead

←Pearl bead

──Bicone bead

Fire-polished bead→

──Pearl bead

←Purchased strap

Crimp bead

Bead tip→

Triangle bead→

Bicone bead
(light blue)→

Pearl bead→

Bicone bead
(purple)→

PURPLE STRAP

Supplies

3-mm bicone crystal beads (12 purple, 32 light blue), 40 2-mm pearl beads (beige), 44 3-mm triangle beads (light green), bead tip, crimp bead, 2 50-cm lengths nylon thread, purchased strap

Instructions

Weave figure eights with 2 strands nylon thread, referring to drawing. Attach a bead tip to all 4 strands at end. Secure with a bead tip and crimp bead; attach purchased strap.

KING'S STRAP

The sparkling crown at the end of this streamlined strap, and the twisted bugle bead accents, create a royal look.

QUEEN'S STRAP

The graceful design and delicate fringe add up to a strap fit for a queen.

KING'S STRAP

Supplies

4-mm bicone crystal beads (2 lavender, 5 rust, 6 light brown), 2 3-mm bicone crystal beads (light brown), 5-mm round fire-polished bead (light green), 5 4-mm round fire-polished beads (pink gold), 6 2 x 12-mm twisted bugle beads (brown), 15 2-mm seed beads (pink silver), crimp bead, nylon thread (2 30-cm lengths, 1 60-cm length), 70-cm nylon wire, purchased strap

Instructions

① Make Motifs a and b. Tie threads; cut excess.
② String beads and motif on wire, referring to drawings. Attach purchased strap with a crimp bead.

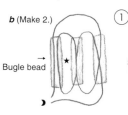

a (Make 1.)

Insert 5-mm fire-polished bead; tie threads.

4-mm bicone bead (light brown)

↑ 4-mm fire-polished bead

★ 4-mm bicone bead (rust)

b (Make 2.)

Bugle bead →

Seed bead

①

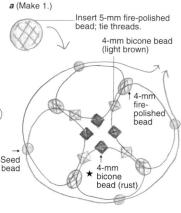

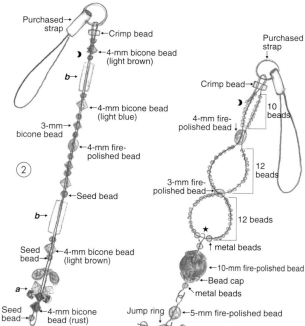

Purchased strap

← Crimp bead

b →

← 4-mm bicone bead (light brown)

← 4-mm bicone bead (light blue)

3-mm → bicone bead

← 4-mm fire-polished bead

②

← Seed bead

b →

Seed bead

← 4-mm bicone bead (light brown)

a →

Seed bead →

← 4-mm bicone bead (rust)

★

Purchased strap

Crimp bead →

10 beads

4-mm fire-polished bead ↓

12 beads

3-mm fire-polished bead →

12 beads

★

↑ metal beads

← 10-mm fire-polished bead

← Bead cap

← metal beads

Jump ring ← 5-mm fire-polished bead

metal beads

Instructions for Queen's Strap are on next page.

62

CRYSTAL STRAP

Supplies

3-mm bicone crystal beads (4 green, 26 crystal), 8-mm round fire-polished bead (light green), 4-mm round fire-polished bead (iridescent green), 51 2-mm seed beads (green), 2.5-cm headpin, 2 2-cm eyepins, crimp bead, 30-cm nylon wire, purchased strap

Instructions

①Weave motif (Figs. A, B). Tie threads; cut excess.

②Make other components, referring to drawings. String all components and beads on wire. Attach purchased strap with crimp bead.

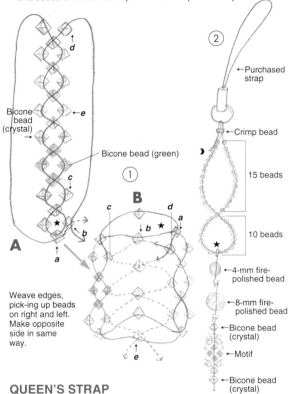

Bicone bead (crystal)

Bicone bead (green)

①

A

B

Weave edges, picking up beads on right and left. Make opposite side in same way.

②

←Purchased strap

←Crimp bead

15 beads

10 beads

★

←4-mm fire-polished bead

←8-mm fire-polished bead

←Bicone bead (crystal)

←Motif

←Bicone bead (crystal)

QUEEN'S STRAP

Supplies

10-mm round fire-polished bead (brown), 5-mm round fire-polished bead (bronze), 4-mm round fire-polished bead (brown), 3-mm round fire-polished bead (bronze), 12 3-mm round metal beads (gold), 68 1.5-mm seed beads (bronze), 2 bead caps, 8 2-cm headpins, eyepins (1 2-cm, 1 4-cm), 4-mm jump ring, crimp bead, 40cm nylon wire, purchased strap

Instructions

String beads on wire, referring to drawing on previous page. Connect components. Attach purchased strap with crimp bead.

CRYSTAL STRAP

The cube-shaped motif, made from large fire-polished beads, is decorated with a lovely bicone-bead star.

Supplies

2 4-mm bicone crystal beads (light pink), 9 3-mm bicone crystal beads (light blue), 4-mm round fire-polished beads (4 lavender, 8 iridescent brown), 2 2-mm round metal beads (bronze), 2-mm seed beads (12 lavender, 48 yellow), bead tip, crimp bead, 2 40-cm lengths nylon thread, purchased strap

Instructions

①Beginning at ★, weave strap. Attach bead tip and crimp bead to end, then purchased strap.

②Weave motif at bottom of strap, adding new beads. Tie threads; cut excess.

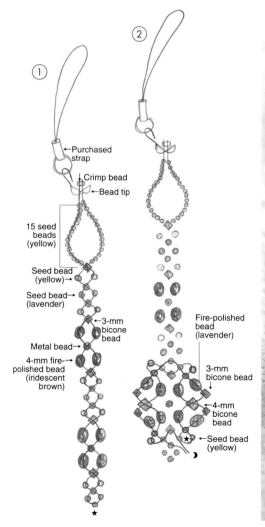

①

←Purchased strap

←Crimp bead

←Bead tip

15 seed beads (yellow)

Seed bead (yellow)→

Seed bead→ (lavender)

←3-mm bicone bead

Metal bead→

4-mm fire-→ polished bead (iridescent brown)

②

Fire-polished bead (lavender)

3-mm bicone bead

←4-mm bicone bead

★←Seed bead (yellow)

FLOWER STRAP

This romantic strap features two flower motifs, one small and one large.

★

64

Supplies

1-cm (length) drop designer bead (black), 2 4-mm bicone crystal beads (black), 6 3-mm bicone crystal beads (black), 5-mm round fire-polished bead (black), 6 4-mm round fire-polished beads (black), 2-mm seed beads (6 silver, 73 black), 2-cm headpin, 2-cm eyepin, 3-mm jump ring, crimp bead, 40-cm nylon wire, purchased strap

Instructions

①Make motif. Tie threads; cut excess.

②Attach other components to motif, referring to drawings. Weave strap with wire, picking up beads from opposite side as you go along. Attach purchased strap with crimp bead.

BLACK STAR STRAP

This strap is all black except for silver beads at the center of the star motif.

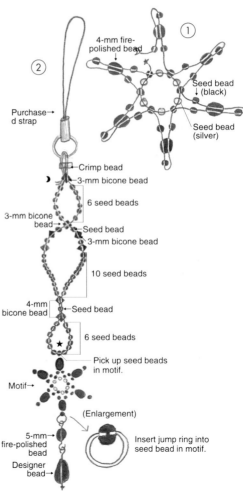

①

4-mm fire-polished bead

Seed bead ↓ (black)

Seed bead (silver)

②

Purchased strap

Crimp bead

3-mm bicone bead

6 seed beads

3-mm bicone bead

Seed bead

3-mm bicone bead

10 seed beads

4-mm bicone bead — Seed bead

6 seed beads

★

Pick up seed beads in motif.

Motif→

(Enlargement)

Insert jump ring into seed bead in motif.

5-mm fire-polished bead

Designer bead→

FLOWER BOBBY PIN

A large flower motif is sewn onto felt to make this dazzling hair ornament.

Supplies

40 3-mm bicone crystal beads (blue), 6-mm round fire-polished bead (bronze), 20 4-mm round fire-polished beads (red), 10 3-mm round fire-polished beads (purple), 10 6-mm bugle beads (green), 1.5-mm seed beads (10 silver, 20 red, 30 green), nylon thread (1 200-cm length, 1 30-cm length), pink embroidery floss, 2 3-cm felt circles (beige), bobby pin with round pad, craft glue

Instructions

①Make motif (Figs. A, B). Tie threads; cut excess.
②Align 2 felt circles and blanket-stitch around edges.
③Place motif on top of felt; attach with nylon thread. Attach 6-mm fire-polished bead at center. Sew only top layer of felt circle.
④Glue motif to pad on bobby pin.

BOBBY PIN WITH LACY DECORATION

Pearl beads are the focus of this design, reminiscent of antique hair ornaments.

Supplies

4 3-mm pearl beads (purple), 8 2-mm pearl beads (pink), 40 1.5-mm seed beads (light brown), 80cm nylon thread, 5.5-cm bobby pin with 2 loops

Instructions

① Insert thread into loop of bobby pin and begin weaving.

② Weave motif, referring to drawings. Pass thread through other loop. Tie threads; cut excess.

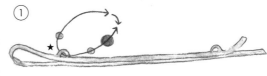

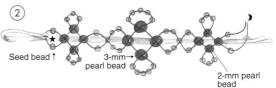

Seed bead ↑   3-mm→ pearl bead   2-mm pearl bead

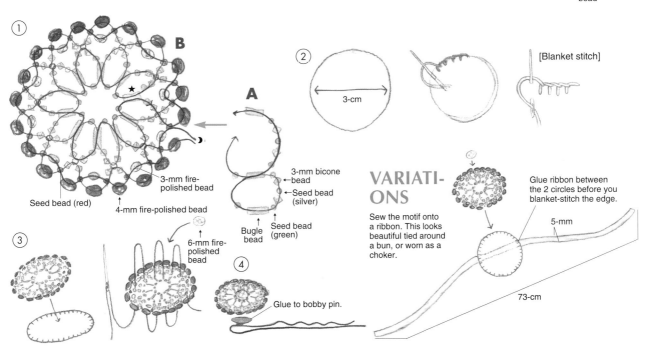

① B

★

← (arrow)

3-mm fire-polished bead

Seed bead (red)   4-mm fire-polished bead

A

② 3-cm   [Blanket stitch]

3-mm bicone bead ←
← Seed bead (silver)
Bugle bead   Seed bead (green)
↑ 6-mm fire-polished bead

③

④ Glue to bobby pin.

VARIATIONS

Sew the motif onto a ribbon. This looks beautiful tied around a bun, or worn as a choker.

Glue ribbon between the 2 circles before you blanket-stitch the edge.

5-mm

73-cm

67

FLORAL PONYTAIL HOLDER

Flower motifs transform an ordinary ponytail holder. Choose beads that complement your hair color.

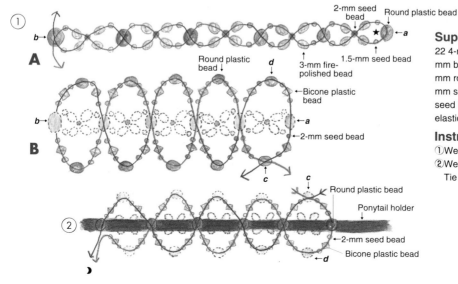

① A

2-mm seed bead
Round plastic bead
1.5-mm seed bead
3-mm fire-polished bead

B
Round plastic bead ↓
d
Bicone plastic bead
2-mm seed bead

c

②
c
Round plastic bead
Ponytail holder
2-mm seed bead
Bicone plastic bead
d

Supplies

22 4-mm round plastic beads (brown), 40 3-mm bicone plastic beads (light brown), 20 3-mm round fire-polished beads (beige), 5 2-mm seed beads (pink silver), 100 1.5-mm seed beads (bronze), 200-cm nylon thread, elastic ponytail holder

Instructions

①Weave motif (Figs. A, B).
②Weave beads around ponytail holder.
  Tie threads; cut excess.

68

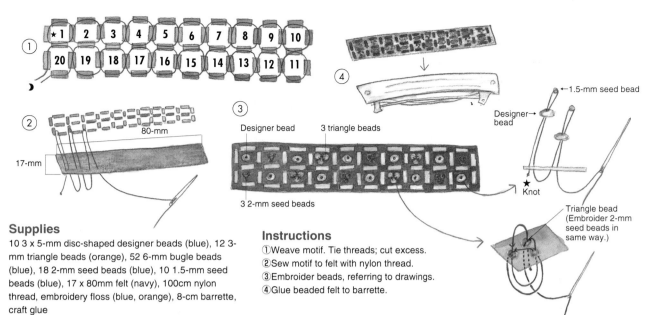

Supplies

10 3 x 5-mm disc-shaped designer beads (blue), 12 3-mm triangle beads (orange), 52 6-mm bugle beads (blue), 18 2-mm seed beads (blue), 10 1.5-mm seed beads (blue), 17 x 80mm felt (navy), 100cm nylon thread, embroidery floss (blue, orange), 8-cm barrette, craft glue

① Weave motif. Tie threads; cut excess.
② Sew motif to felt with nylon thread.
③ Embroider beads, referring to drawings.
④ Glue beaded felt to barrette.

Figure labels

- 80-mm
- 17-mm
- Designer bead
- 3 triangle beads
- 3 2-mm seed beads
- 1.5-mm seed bead
- Designer bead
- ★ Knot
- Triangle bead (Embroider 2-mm seed beads in same way.)

Instructions

BEADED BARRETTE

To make this barrette, you simply make a framework from bugle beads, attach it to a piece of felt, and sew the beads on.

Supplies

9 6 x 8-mm designer oval beads (bronze), 36 3-mm bicone crystal beads (light brown), 20 4-mm round fire-polished beads (light gray), 10 6-mm pearl beads (beige), 36 2-mm pearl beads (pink), 18 3-mm triangle beads (light brown), 18 3-mm bugle beads (purple), 1.8-mm three-cut beads (20 gold, 150 brown), 2 5-mm jump rings, 2 bead tips, 2 crimp beads, 90cm nylon wire, 2 eyeglass holders

Instructions

String beads, referring to drawings. Attach a bead tip and crimp bead to each end. Attach eyeglass holders to both ends with jump rings.

PEARL-AND-BRONZE EYEGLASS CHAIN

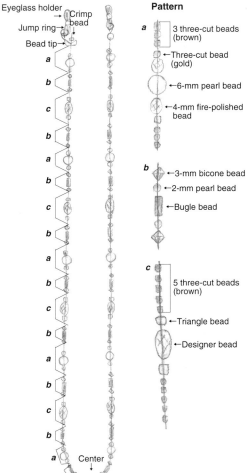

Eyeglass holder
Jump ring
Crimp bead
Bead tip

a
b
c
b
a
b
c
b
a
b
c
b
a
b
c
b
a
b
c
b
a
b
c

Center

Pattern

a
3 three-cut beads (brown)
←Three-cut bead (gold)
←6-mm pearl bead
←4-mm fire-polished bead

b
←3-mm bicone bead
←2-mm pearl bead
←Bugle bead

c
5 three-cut beads (brown)
←Triangle bead
←Designer bead

EYEGLASS CHAINS

Multicolored EYEGLASS CHAIN

This elegant eyeglass chain features faceted-glass beads in a variety of colors, styles and sizes, with pearl and triangle bead accents.

Supplies

5 4 x 6-mm oval designer beads (brown), 4-mm bicone crystal beads (12 each purple, wine, violet), 6 5-mm round fire-polished beads (brown), 10 4-mm round fire-polished beads (orange), 10 3-mm round fire-polished beads (purple), 2-mm pearl beads (10 red, 20 lavender), 22 3-mm triangle beads (orange), 352 1.5-mm seed beads (red), 2 5-mm jump rings, 2 bead tips, 2 crimp beads, 90cm nylon wire, eyeglass holders

Instructions

String beads, referring to drawings. Attach a bead tip and crimp bead to each end. Attach eyeglass holders with jump rings.

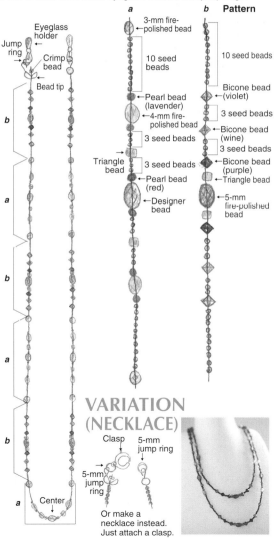

VARIATION (NECKLACE)

Or make a necklace instead. Just attach a clasp.

MINIATURE PURSE

This exquisite design features two floral motifs. Attach it to your handbag or belt with a chain. Place some solid perfume inside it, and the fragrance will waft wherever you walk.

OTHER ACCESSORIES

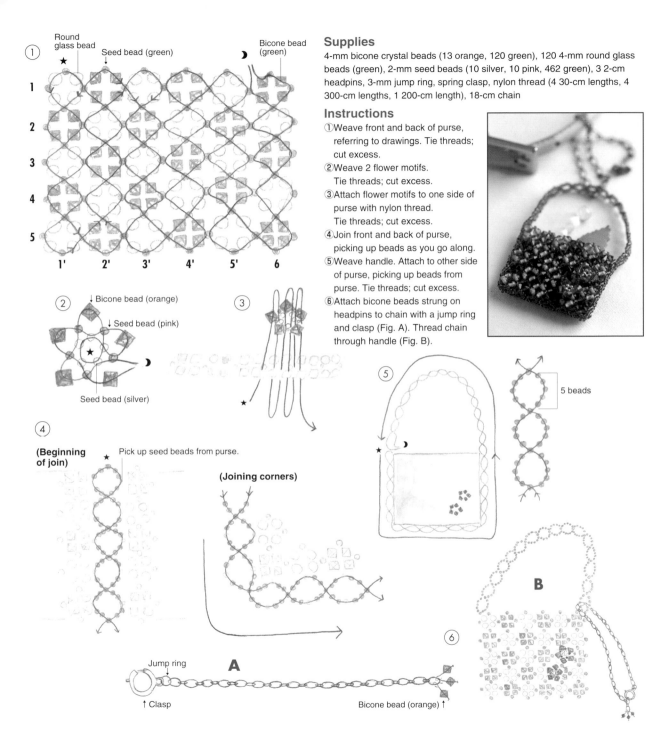

① Round glass bead ★   Seed bead (green) ↓   Bicone bead (green) ☽

1
2
3
4
5

1' 2' 3' 4' 5' 6

② ↓ Bicone bead (orange)   ↓ Seed bead (pink)   ★
Seed bead (silver)

③ ★

Supplies

4-mm bicone crystal beads (13 orange, 120 green), 120 4-mm round glass beads (green), 2-mm seed beads (10 silver, 10 pink, 462 green), 3 2-cm headpins, 3-mm jump ring, spring clasp, nylon thread (4 30-cm lengths, 4 300-cm lengths, 1 200-cm length), 18-cm chain

Instructions

① Weave front and back of purse, referring to drawings. Tie threads; cut excess.

② Weave 2 flower motifs. Tie threads; cut excess.

③ Attach flower motifs to one side of purse with nylon thread. Tie threads; cut excess.

④ Join front and back of purse, picking up beads as you go along.

⑤ Weave handle. Attach to other side of purse, picking up beads from purse. Tie threads; cut excess.

⑥ Attach bicone beads strung on headpins to chain with a jump ring and clasp (Fig. A). Thread chain through handle (Fig. B).

⑤   5 beads

④ (Beginning of join)   ★   Pick up seed beads from purse.

(Joining corners)

A   Jump ring   ↑ Clasp   Bicone bead (orange) ↑

B

⑥

BROOCH WITH MINIATURE PURSE

This bright blue, fringed miniature purse is attached to a pin back so that you can fasten it anywhere you like.

Supplies

50 5 x 10-mm oval plastic beads (blue), 2 3 x 5-mm rectangular designer beads (blue), 18 3-mm round fire-polished beads (olive), 5 2-mm pearl beads (white), 500 1.8-mm three-cut beads (green), 3 2-cm headpins, 8 2-cm eyepins, 15mm (diameter) perforated pin back, nylon thread (1 400-cm length, 2 100-cm lengths, 1 30-cm length, 2 20-cm lengths)

Instructions

①Weave 3 rows to make purse, referring to drawings. Tie threads; cut excess.
②Weave bottom of purse. Tie threads; cut excess.
③Weave clasp and fringe, referring to drawings.
④Attach beads to perforated pin back (Figs. A-E). Tie threads on inside of pin back; cut excess. Insert a headpin into pin back from inside; round end (Fig. F). Cut tabs on bottom of pin back in half and attach to top.
⑤Join brooch and purse, referring to drawings.

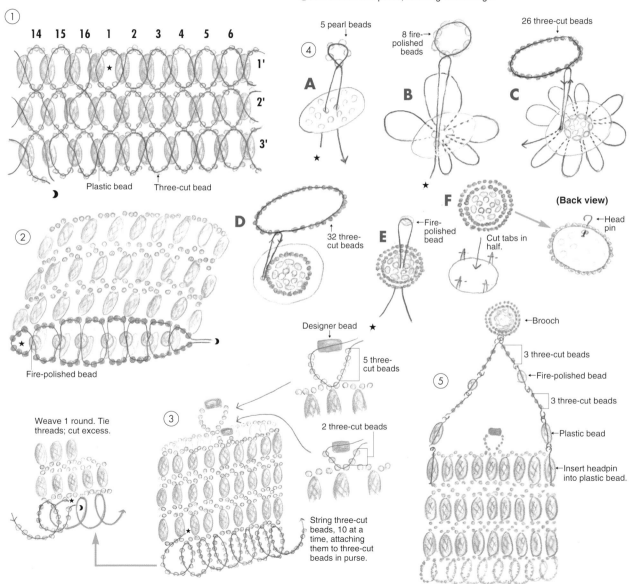

75

MAGNET CARD HOLDER

Decorate magnets to make an elegant card holder. You'll need two for a standard-size card, and four for a large one.

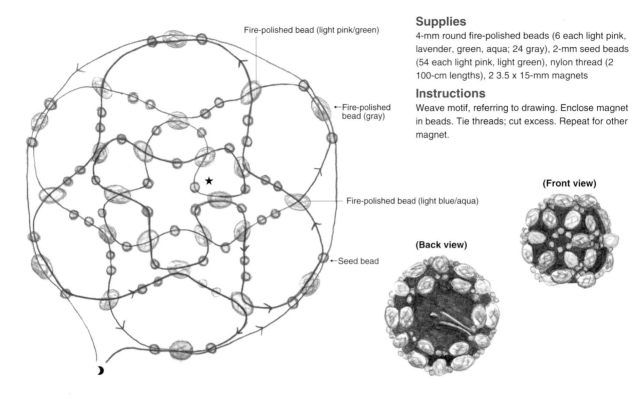

Fire-polished bead (light pink/green)

←Fire-polished bead (gray)

Fire-polished bead (light blue/aqua)

←Seed bead

Supplies

4-mm round fire-polished beads (6 each light pink, lavender, green, aqua; 24 gray), 2-mm seed beads (54 each light pink, light green), nylon thread (2 100-cm lengths), 2 3.5 x 15-mm magnets

Instructions

Weave motif, referring to drawing. Enclose magnet in beads. Tie threads; cut excess. Repeat for other magnet.

(Front view)

(Back view)

BEADS

Beads are available in an amazingly wide range of sizes, shapes, colors and materials. On these two pages, we show all the types of beads used for the projects in this book.

Bicone crystal beads

Round fire-polished beads

Round beads faceted-glass beads

Faceted glass beads

Faceted-glass beads have cut surfaces that reflect light beautifully. In this book, we use three types: bicone crystal beads, round fire-polished beads and round faceted-glass beads.

Drop beads

Round and oval beads

Triangle beads

2-mm seed beads

5-mm seed beads

3-mm seed beads

1.5-mm seed beads

Drop beads

These beads have holes in the top. They add texture and dimension to a piece.

Round or oval glass beads

The surfaces of these glass beads are uncut.

Triangle beads

These three-sided beads with rounded edges add sparkle to any piece.

Seed beads

Seed beads are tiny cylindrical beads with large holes. They are available in a fairly wide range of sizes, and are the beads most often used in bead jewelry and accessories.

Rhinestones

Rhinestones in settings can be strung like beads. Flat and diamond-shaped rhinestones are attached with glue.

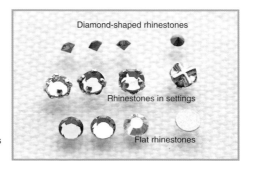

Diamond-shaped rhinestones

Rhinestones in settings

Flat rhinestones

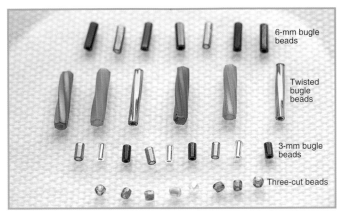

6-mm bugle beads

Twisted bugle beads

3-mm bugle beads

Three-cut beads

Bugle beads

The most commonly used form of bugle beads is the 3-mm size, but longer ones (6mm) are also available, as are twisted bugle beads.

Three-cut beads

Three-cut beads come in the same range of sizes as seed beads. They add brilliance to a piece, as the irregular cuts on their surfaces reflect light beautifully.

Designer beads

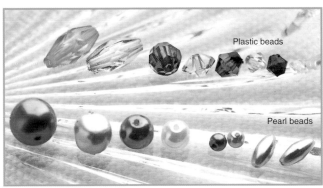

Gemstone beads

Freshwater pearl beads

Gemstone beads

Gemstone beads, such as citrine and amethyst, are made from minerals or petrified minerals. Some are cut into specific shapes; others are used in their natural state.

Freshwater pearl beads

These beads are made by drilling holes in freshwater pearls. They are available in a surprisingly wide range of colors.

Designer beads

Designer beads come in many shapes, sizes and colors. Some are inspired by nature (flowers, leaves and birds). Others are more abstract. They are usually used as accents or focal points.

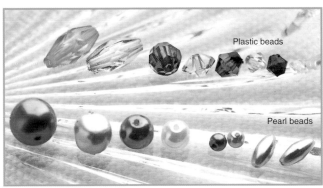

Plastic beads

Pearl beads

Plastic beads

These lightweight beads are now available in a wide range of colors, shapes and sizes.

Pearl beads

These are plastic beads made to look like pearls. Their large holes make them ideal for stringing.

Metal beads

Metal beads

These are usually made of base metal, which is sometimes plated with precious metals, but you'll also find gold and silver-filled beads.

BASIC INSTRUCTIONS

In this section, we introduce the basic techniques used in making bead jewelry. Though they may at first seem a bit complex, mastering them will make your work easier and more enjoyable. With just these techniques, you can make almost any type of jewelry. We also describe the tools and findings you will be using.

WEAVING FIGURE EIGHTS

This is the most basic weaving technique. As you string beads, you form intersections in them with nylon thread. You can apply this technique to make most types of jewelry.

1
String beads on center of nylon thread. The pink bead is at the center, and the blue beads are on either side of it.

2
String a new bead and form a left-right intersection by passing the other end of nylon thread through it. Thread should extend from both sides of the new bead.

3
Add a bead on each side of bead circle (blue beads in photo).

4
Add a new bead and form an intersection in it. You now have two circles, resembling a figure eight. Continue weaving, repeating this pattern.

Closing the circle

1
Photo shows a series of woven figure eights.

2
Form an intersection in first bead strung with nylon thread.

3
Pull thread to close circle.

4
Closed circle.

Weaving the next row

1
At end of first row, form an intersection in a bead in the direction in which you will be working (upward).

2
String beads on second row as shown in photo at left.

3
Form an intersection in a bead facing the direction in which you will be working (right).

4
Continue weaving in the same way, picking up beads from first row.

TOOLS AND AUXILIARY MATERIALS

Nylon thread, wire
These are used to string beads. Nylon thread is flexible and strong. Nylon-coated or stainless-steel wire is best for pieces that require more rigidity (necklaces, for instance).
◆Sizes used for the projects in this book◆
Nylon thread: #1.5-#2
Nylon-coated wire: 0.24-0.36mm
Stainless-steel wire: 0.2-0.3mm

Flat-nose pliers, round-nose pliers, wire-cutters
These tools are used when you work with wire, headpins or eyepins, and findings. Flat-nose pliers (shown at right in three styles) are used to compress crimp beads, bead tips and perforated pin or earring backs. Round-nose pliers (bottom left) are used to round the ends of headpins or eyepins. Wire-cutters (top left) are used to cut headpins and eyepins, and wire.

🔷 FINISHING TECHNIQUES 🔷

In most cases, pieces made with nylon thread are finished by tying thread ends together. The ends of stainless-steel wire can be twisted together. Use crimp beads at the ends of pieces that cannot be twisted or tied.

Tying nylon thread

1 Tie thread ends together. If ends are not in same location, pass one of them through beads until it is close enough to the other to tie.

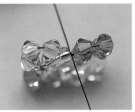

2 Tie tightly 2-3 times to secure. Photograph shows threads tied between beads.

3 Pass one thread end through adjacent beads.

4 Pull thread tightly so that knot slips under a bead. Cut excess thread at the edge of a bead.

Twisting stainless-steel wire

1 If ends of wire are not in same location, pass one of them through beads until it is close enough to the other to twist.

2 Align 2 strands of wire and twist 3-4 times. For best results, twist with flat-nose pliers or a similar tool.

3 Cut wire with wire-cutters, leaving 2-3mm twisted wire.

4 Bend twisted wires down with flat pliers so they won't scratch your skin.

Using a crimp bead to finish a piece made with nylon wire

1 String crimp bead on wire, then any beads that need to be strung past it. Pass wire back through beads to crimp bead.

2 Making sure wire is taut, compress crimp bead with flat-nose pliers. If you're using nylon thread, compress the crimp bead gently so you don't cut the thread.

3 String remaining beads, then follow Steps 1-2 in reverse order. Cut excess wire.

Beading needles
These are good to have on hand when you're using fine nylon thread, or when you're passing nylon thread through the same beads many times. Since they are designed to accommodate even tiny beads, beading needles are thinner than ordinary sewing needles.

Glue
Applied to knots in nylon thread and compressed crimp beads. We recommend two-part epoxy. Avoid superglue, because it tends to discolor beads.

Ring stick
Ring sticks are used by jewelers to size rings. It's good to have one of these to check measurements as you work.

ATTACHING CLASPS AND ADJUSTABLE CHAIN CLOSURES

Attaching clasps with crimp beads

1
String clasp and crimp bead on one end of wire, as shown in photo at left. Compress crimp bead with flat-nose pliers.

2
There should be a 1-2mm space between crimp bead and clasp. Continue stringing beads.

3
String crimp bead and adjustable chain closure on other end of wire. Compress crimp bead; cut excess wire with wire-cutters.

Attaching clasps with bead tips

1
Close bead tip with flat-nose pliers. Attach to clasp with a jump ring.

2
Attach adjustable chain closure to bead tip. Close with flat-nose pliers.

Attaching bead tips

1
String bead tip, then crimp bead on wire or thread.

2
Adjust tension by pulling on wire. Compress crimp bead with flat pliers.

3
Leaving a 1-2-mm end extending from crimp bead, cut wire with wire-cutters. Close bead tip with flat pliers.

4
There should be a 1-mm space between bead tip and strung beads.

Working with jump rings

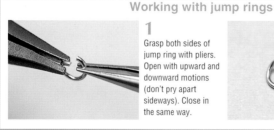

1
Grasp both sides of jump ring with pliers. Open with upward and downward motions (don't pry apart sideways). Close in the same way.

2
Attach findings to opened jump ring.

FINDINGS
Most of the findings used for the projects in this book are shown on these two pages. Learning how to work with them will broaden the range of pieces you can make.

Crimp beads
(See instructions on pp. 81-82.)

Bead tips
(See instructions above.)

Spring clasp (right)
Adjustable chain closure (left)
(See instructions above.)

Other clasps
Toggle and other types of clasps can be used instead of a spring clasp and adjustable chain closure.

Jump rings
(See instructions above.)
◆Sizes used for the jewelry in this book:◆
3-3.5mm, 4mm, 5mm

⬦ WORKING WITH HEADPINS AND EYEPINS ⬦

String beads onto headpins or eyepins, round ends and attach to other components.
Since both ends of eyepins can be rounded, they can be combined to form a chain.

Working with perforated findings

Perforated findings provide a good foundation for beadwork with some volume.

Rounding ends of headpins

1 String beads on headpin, leaving 7-8mm at end. Cut excess with wire-cutters.

2 Bend headpin at a right angle near hole in bead.

3 Round end of headpin with round-nose pliers. Begin rounding at end of headpin.

4 Round end until it forms an attractive circle right up against edge of bead.

5 Photo at left shows examples of headpins that have been rounded incorrectly.

Rounding ends of eyepins

Follow procedure for rounding ends of headpins shown at left. Make sure circles at ends are the same size, and face the same direction. For some pieces, ends may be bent at a 90E angle (inward).

Connecting headpins and eyepins

1 Open rounded pin, pulling it to the front and back.

2 Attach to another component.

3 Close circle with flat-nose pliers.

1 To avoid marring beads or breaking nylon thread, cut tabs in half.

2 Bend two adjacent tabs down with flat-nose pliers, using a folding motion.

3 After attaching beads to finding, slide the two sections together, catching the bent tabs.

4 Bend remaining tabs down. Place a tissue between pliers and finding to protect beads and thread.

5 Completed piece

Headpins (left)
Eyepins (right)
(See instructions above.)
Pins used for the projects in this book measure 0.6-0.7mm in diameter.

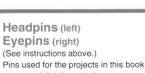

Perforated findings
(See instructions above.)
Perforated pin backs and rings are also available.

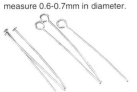

Bead caps
These are decorative findings that cover one end of a bead. Choose a size that fits the beads you are using.

Ear wires

Necklace clamp
Used to secure ends of ribbon. Choose a size to match width of ribbon you are using.

83

SAMEJIMA Takako
Jewelry designer

Born in Tokyo in 1970, Ms. Samejima has been fascinated by beads since her elementary school days. Though at first she referred to craft books, she is largely self-taught. After graduating from high school, she became a beautician, but spent most of her spare time making bead jewelry. Demand for her creations increased. In 1995, Ms. Samejima opened a studio she named Crystalloid, and began a new career as a jewelry designer. Her colorful, sophisticated pieces have been featured in many fashion magazines. She is also the author of *My Beaded Accessories, Sweet Bead Collection and Pure Beads in Japanese.*